I Am NOT a Desperate Housewife

I Am NOT *a Desperate Housewife*

A Homeland Security Plan for Desperate Times

LaVerne Farmer

I Am Not a Desperate Housewife

©2007 by LaVerne Farmer

ISBN-13: 978-1-4243-2323-4
ISBN-10: 1-4243-2323-1

Edited by Fran Carter
Cover Photograph by Gosden, GVPStudio2
Design by TextStyles

All Scripture quotations are taken from the
King James Version of the Bible

Printed in the United States of America

For information:
Motherhood Evangelisms, Inc.
5604 Warrenshire Dr.
West Bloomfield, Michigan 48322

www. motherhoodevangelisms.org

Dedicated to my husband Darryl,
my children LaVette, Darryl II, Nicole and Brian
Whom I Love with All My Heart

To my loving wife, LaVerne:

This is an unusual, yet altogether fitting acknowledgment of an unusual and anointed woman of God.

For those who will doubtless become captivated by the mere title of this book . . .

You Are Not Alone!

For those inquiring minds who want to know if . . .

The unequivocal answer is . . .

NO! My wife is not a desperate housewife.

What she is, though, is very anointed in her calling, very spiritual in her devotions, very adventurous in her walk of faith.

Most importantly, she is very sincere, with a commitment to accomplish the impossible. But then, nothing is impossible with God, and if God be for you, who can be against you.

I have had the honor and pleasure for the past twenty-five years of loving my wife and family and sharing in the commitment to help develop and deepen their love for God.

Read the book and continue the good fight of faith in Christ Jesus.

Minister D.E. Farmer, Sr.

Contents

Perceptions

"Oh, I'm just a housewife". Throughout decades this has been the cliché of millions of women, who by fact of experience realize that there is nothing simple or effortless about being a housewife. For years society has further diminished the role of the home maker to stereotypes portrayed by women on television whose most authoritative warnings were predicated on, "Wait 'till your father gets home". In recent years, Hollywood has made an extreme contradiction to the 1950's stigmas with their portrayal of housewives as self absorbed adulteresses whose main agenda is maintaining their social position in their community social status totem pole. NOT! These extremes may be someone's reality, but as born again believers we do not ascribe to this propaganda. We have a higher calling. We don't allow the world to define who we are and what we do. We are women individually assigned to specific purposes for the building of the kingdom of God, and our divinely maintained relationship with Jesus Christ affords us specific daily strategies for home, church, and the community around us.

> We have no intention of backing away from any threat that tries to endanger our marriage, home, or family.

We are Kingdom builders. We reflect Christ in our walk, talk, and daily interactions with others. We are praying women, influenced by the Holy Ghost as to how and what to pray. We pray for husbands, families, leaders and the people with whom they come in contact! We pray that the Word of God will manifest "Thy kingdom come and Thy will be done on earth as it is in heaven" (Matthew 6:10). Make no mistake, we are women driven to "hold down the fort", maintain the victory and benefits wrought for us by the works of the cross.

God has given directives to ask, seek, and knock, (Luke 11:9) to receive and distribute the rewards of being on His side. We have no intention of backing away from any threat that tries to endanger our marriage, home, or family. God has promised us abundant life and we will defy every thought, word or deed that speaks to the contrary. We know how to fight the "Good fight of faith", (1 Timothy 6:12) in a meek and quiet spirit (I Peter 3:1) and maintain beauty and sophistication while doing it!

I Am NOT a Desperate Housewife

ONE

Our Time Is Come

Kings of armies did flee apace: and she that tarried at home divided the spoil.

Though ye have lien among the pots, yet shall ye be as the wings of a dove covered with silver, and her feathers with yellow gold (Psalm 68:12–13).

As Lord and Savior, Jesus Christ has cleansed us from sin, driven demonic strongholds out from their position of authority and redeemed every born again believer back to Him to an assigned purpose in the Kingdom of God. This redemption includes assignments for housewives whose past in most cultures and religious sects bore a stigma of insignificance which still continues unto this day.

Interestingly enough Christian housewives have been entrusted with incredible tasks to birth, nurture and train the next generation of believers as well as disperse the benefits from both current and past spiritual victories. Trained by faith, mixed with the Word, (Hebrew 4:2) these God given assignments have been the Spiritual validations of the anointed Christian housewife of yesterday and today.

3

We have our assignments and the tools with which we are to complete them; there are to be no substitutes. We must have faith substantiated in the Word of God, to identify the tactics of the enemy, destroy his influences and take hold of every possession, promise and blessing that has been stolen by blind siding deception. Ephesians 1:3 tells us:

> *Blessed be the God and Father of our Lord Jesus Christ, who hath blessed us with all spiritual blessings in heavenly places in Christ.*

We are provided with all the spiritual blessings that we will ever need. The Word of God reveals the hidden treasures and gives authority to take hold of all that God has provided us. Jesus paved the way in Colossians 2:15:

> *And having spoiled principalities and powers, he made a shew of them openly, triumphing over them in it.*

Our stuff is being held captive by a powerless enemy. Jesus took away all authority from the enemy, and now all the enemy can do is bluff. Call his bluff, and take back your stuff! Get it! Maintain and share it!

We have unlimited access to the Kingdom of God through His Word. Most of us have experienced the access; it is the living and maintaining of these kingdom principles we find more difficult. It is vitally important to our spiritual development that we through the Word of God learn how to maintain sustained victories, for this is how we facilitate the properly dispersing to others the knowledge we've *experienced* in the Word of God.

Jesus took away all authority from the enemy, and now all the enemy can do is bluff. Call his bluff, and take back your stuff!

God has given us a mandate to give. We do not receive just for ourselves, but our gifts, talents, and rewards are for the body of Christ. God rewards us with exceeding precious promises. Along with these rewards is the responsibility of sharing these physical and spiritual blessings with others. It is paramount in receiving and dispersing rewards to maintain spiritual momentum and sensitivity so we can hear specifically to whom God would have us give.

TWO

Mastering the Mundane

It may not seem to be monumental; in fact, it tends to lend itself to drudgery. You know! The everyday, the routine, and the infinite lists of things to do. Things that no one else really appreciates, thanks you for, or even considers helping you with; "the mommy/housewife stuff".

You stand back and think about your education, how far you've advanced up the corporate ladder, your beauty and charm, and you realize that your astute problem solving skills have been diminished to, "how did that get on the bathroom wall?"

Don't despair, we've all been there! The key to getting out of there is predicated upon how you allow the Lord to influence your view of the situation. Life is filled with mastering the mundane; it is part of the process. It is imperative that we "master the moment" and not allow our emotions to master us. We are leaders; we are setting an example for our children. Our children are to see us pray, praise,

> . . . and you realize that your astute problem solving skills have been diminished to, "how did that get on the bathroom wall?"

and worship God in church, at home, and during our family devotion. They should see those prayers at work, as we practice being calm in those every day family crises. We need to look at the activities of our day as lessons to be learned, and make them opportunities to demonstrate the "fruits of the spirit" (Galatians 5:22, 23).

Your spouse is rewarded with your peace. He draws from it, looks forward to it, and has come to depend on it. It is a crazy and hectic world. The workplace is filled with unregenerate souls who have mastered the skills in self preservation. We must create a sanctuary, a place of peace for our husbands that they find comfort in coming home to our constants of order, clean house, dinner, and tranquility. Not to say that this happens every day, but it is a practice and a goal for the norm.

Likewise, our children are subjected daily to the cruelty of classmates, the frustration of teachers in overcrowded classrooms, not fitting in and not quite understanding why. Seeing you at home, welcoming them, loving them, and being concerned about what concerns them can heal some of their worst days.

Taking the right attitude causes us to be a blessing to our families, and when we bless our family, God blesses us.

When my children were younger, I participated in their school's PTA and the community housing association. At that particular time one of the main focuses was establishing "safe houses". These were homes that were designated as safe places for a child to take refuge in cases of emergency or instances where the child and/or their surroundings seemed threatening. As mothers, we are to take responsibility for making sure that we do our part in providing a spiritual safe haven for our children. We must watch as well as pray, keeping our spiritual eyes open for the faintest signals of approaching problems for the Bible tells us it is "the little foxes that spoil the vine: for our vines have tender grapes" (Song of Solomon 2:15). At home we provide our children with nutrition, security and stability, they are young and impressionable and we cannot allow the enemy to entice them away from the Biblical foundation upon which they are raised.

The enemy tries to sneak in subtlety through friends, television, movies and music to snatch them from the "vine" that has been the source of their sustenance. We must keep a watch and discern any changes in their spiritual appetite and behavior and immediately address them in the spirit so we can know what and how to lodge a counter attack.

Only God can really reward us and make us feel good about accomplishing the mundane. It's very natural to feel as though you are the hired help with a forfeited pay, but rest assured, pay day will come in the spiritual and physical, if not now, then later. In order to realize the reward you must decide that God is the real recipient of your daily actions. Such actions are a component of your "living sacrifice". This living sacrifice is to be presented "holy and acceptable unto God" (Romans 12:1). Whether it is sweeping the floor, witnessing to a neighbor or reading a bedtime story, don't resent it, because the right attitude is the catalyst for receiving from God more than you deserve!

This Includes You!

> But God hath chosen the foolish things of the world to confound the wise; and God hath chosen the weak things of the world to confound the things which are mighty; And base things of the world, and things which are despised, hath God chosen, yea, and things which are not, to bring to nought things that are:
> That no flesh should glory in his presence. But of him are ye in Christ Jesus, who of God is made unto us wisdom, and righteousness, and

sanctification, and redemption: That, according
as it is written, He that glorieth, let him glory in
the Lord (1 Corinthians 1:27–31).

The Bible has consistently given us examples of how God chooses again and again the "least expected" to manifest the "exceeding abundantly above". In most religious arenas housewives are considered part of the "least expected". We are taught to teach Sunday and Vacation Bible School, sing in the choir, cook in the kitchen and volunteer for the bake sale. This is great, but we must realize that our walk with Christ cannot be limited to church volunteerism just because we said "I do". In fact, when a believer marries another believer they become a united front and a more eminent threat to the enemy. Christian marriages are automatically enlisted into "spiritual special armed forces" and mandate that you take your relationship with Christ to the next dimension. Consider yourself warned, you'd better put some armor on under that apron, and swing that Sword.

> Holy Ghost filled housewives are a special group of Christians assigned to the "special ops" of Kingdom building; we oftentimes fight in obscurity

Holy Ghost filled housewives are a special group of Christians assigned to the "special ops" of Kingdom building; we oftentimes fight in obscurity, a thankless job, but that's what we do! We have learned to take preventative measures to maintain the spiritual stability of the home. We're not waiting to exhale because part of our training has been how to hold our breath. For when the enemy comes in like a flood, we have learned to inhale the breath of life, hold it and not let go.

Silently watching and praying is mandatory for preventing attacks that can consume our households. Our "modus operandi" is "wise as serpents and harmless as doves" (Matthew 10:16b). Praying in tongues is downloading revelation from heaven and getting answers to questions and situations that have occurred, are occurring, and/or will occur.

We serve a mighty God who is waiting with solutions, ready to answer and give revelation knowledge concerning every situation that concerns our life. We must first realize no matter how apparent certain situations may appear, that we don't always know what to pray. Romans 8:26 tells us;

> *Likewise the Spirit also helpeth our infirmities: for we know not what we should pray for as we ought: but the Spirit itself maketh intercession for us with groanings which cannot be uttered.*

A spirit of humility; the recognition that we are but flesh and blood mortal, serving an omniscient God who knows all things, along with obedience gives us our access to the wisdom of God. A proper flow of wisdom is sustained by the stance that God receives all the glory for all the things He does as we yield ourselves as "instruments of righteousness unto God" (Romans 6:13). Philippians 2:19 reminds us:

> *For it is God which worketh in you both to will and to do of his good pleasure."*

The focus must always remain on God and must be established as;

> *Not by might, nor by power, but by my spirit, saith the LORD of hosts* (Zechariah 4:6b).

He deserves ALL the Glory and ALL the Honor and ALL the Praise for All the success that He has caused us to experience in our lives.

God's eyes are upon us and when we align ourselves to His Word it creates an opportunity for God to "shew Himself strong" (2 Chronicles 16:9) with mighty acts of deliverances. Housewives have often been perceived as minuscule and of little importance. Yes, we are married women and our natural assignments are to take care of our homes, husbands and children, but this mandate does not entitle us to be ignorant of our spiritual responsibilities.

"Morphed"

God has provided us with a wonderful conversion. His Word transforms us from self-consciousness to God consciousness. We are not limited to a role defined by a secular society. We have an enlarged paradigm, we expect more and we get more. We are made in "His image" (Genesis 1:27) with God's likes and His dislikes. We have developed a sophisticated spiritual palette, an appetite for the things of God. We've been exposed to a more refined taste; we no longer settle for off the rack works, we expect custom made blessings, specifically tailor made for us.

It's not that we can afford it and we could never do enough to deserve it, it is purely predicated upon how God feel about us. He tells us how He feels as He whispers His most private thoughts toward us in some of the most public places. "He blesses us 'til we blush". He loves us so much that He gives us:

> . . . *beauty for ashes, the oil of joy for mourning, the garment of praise for the spirit of heaviness; that they might be called trees of righteousness, the planting of the LORD, that he might be glorified* (Isaiah 61:3).

He makes us beautiful both inside and out as we respond to the promise,

Delight thyself also in the LORD; and he shall give thee the desires of thine heart (Psalm 37:4).

Along with the things you've just thought about, God will give you things that you never thought you would ever have. He will give you a desire for things that are indicative of being the heiress you are and His generosity will cause you to be generous.

Deuteronomy 8:18 tells us the purpose of this wealth:

But thou shalt remember the LORD thy God: for it is he that giveth thee power to get wealth, that he may establish his covenant which he sware unto thy fathers, as it is this day."

God gives to us to establish His promises and prove to the entire world, that:

. . . God hath chosen the foolish things of the world to confound the wise; and God hath chosen the weak things of the world to confound the things which are mighty; And base things of the world, and things which are despised, hath God chosen, yea, and things which are not, to bring to nought things that are: that no flesh should glory in his presence" (1 Corinthians 1:27–29).

ALWAYS REMEMBER!
You Are A Threat To the Enemy.

The enemy is always looking for ways to lodge attacks of deception. You wake up and try to figure out what's wrong! Why this sense of lethargic complacency? Why can't I get it together today? There is an easy answer; the enemy wants to bring chaos to your endeavors manifested by God's order. Simple tasks like making a list, making a bed, taking the clothes to the cleaners jump at you all at once, and the next thing you know you feel like there is no way you can get all these things done. Step back, recognize the attack as being an attack of the enemy and realize the goal is to get it done, but not all at one time.

God has grace that is more than sufficient for all of His daily instructions and tasks.

Keep an "Attitude of Gratitude"

It is not enough to just recognize the enemy's strategy; you must also counter his attack by launching the weapon of praise. Begin to praise God for the grace to accomplish every little task no matter how minute. While making that bed pray and tell God:

> *Thank you for giving me the mind to make this bed and not put it off, thank you for grace that gives me order and direction on how to go about knocking each task off my list. Because of you I have a grateful heart and I look forward to my day today and being led by your Spirit and getting done the things you would have me to get done.*

BAMMM! In two minutes you've just launched an assault missile that destroyed the threat of an oppressive weapon of deception.

Oppression Must Be Destroyed!

Isaiah 10:27 says:

> *And it shall come to pass in that day, that his burden shall be taken away from off thy shoulder, and his yoke from off thy neck, and the yoke shall be destroyed because of the anointing.*

THREE

Deception Exposed!

. . . He was a murderer from the beginning, and abode not in the truth, because there is no truth in him. When he speaketh a lie, he speaketh of his own: for he is a liar, and the father of it (John 8:44).

And the serpent said unto the woman, Ye shall not surely die: For God doth know that in the day ye eat thereof, then your eyes shall be opened, and ye shall be as gods, knowing good and evil. And when the woman saw that the tree was good for food, and that it was pleasant to the eyes, and a tree to be desired to make one wise, she took of the fruit thereof, and did eat, and gave also unto her husband with her; and he did eat (Genesis 3:4–6).

Since the beginning the strategy of the enemy has been to torment women with deception and lies, but no longer. The enemy has been EXPOSED. We no longer submit or yield our thoughts, will and emotions to his trickery. The infiltration into our thought life has been identified and we now cast down and destroy enemy strong-holds by use of the Word of God through the power of the Holy Ghost. We stand guard with the sword of the Spirit our weapon of choice to prevent any future deceptive influence.

FOUR

The Deception: "I'm Desperate"

> *Come unto me, all ye that labour and are heavy laden, and I will give you rest. Take my yoke upon you, and learn of me; for I am meek and lowly in heart: and ye shall find rest unto your souls. For my yoke is easy, and my burden is light* (Matthew 11:28–30).

Desperation refers to the conditions of extreme anxiety, worry, hopelessness and fear. It is not unusual for housewives who are concerned for husbands, families, households, and careers to have exemplified one or two of these emotions at some point and time. It is when we habitually practice these emotions on a regular basis, that we find ourselves in trouble and having issues of desperation. God is provident and has never intended for us to rely upon our own limited ingenuity. His Word provides us with knowledge that expels fears of futility and faith that motivates and encourages a trust in God and His plan for our life. Home is not a bad word, and looking to the welfare of those inside the home is not to be chaotic or viewed as an ambitionless occupation. God's home assignments are not any less important than any of His other assignments and they as well, require a complete commitment and willingness to be directed by His instructions.

Not being comfortable with your home assignment may be an indication of the presence of a deceptive influence that's trying to convince you that you are missing out on life and that you should be doing something more productive. Don't despise your current assignment; it is a necessary component in your spiritual development to fulfill the purpose and destiny God has for your life. Ecclesiastes 3:1 says:

> To every thing there is a season, and a time to
> every purpose under the heaven:

> Don't despise your current assignment; it is a necessary component in your spiritual development to fulfill the purpose and destiny God has for your life.

Stay tuned to God and the grace He affords for all our daily activities because home assignments may appear hectic, but operating outside of your assignment is the catalyst for acts of desperation.

Even when it seems as though none of the plans for the day were accomplished due to a barrage of rescue missions and firefighting, take comfort, for firefighters have similar days; they just look at it differently. They realize that they have been trained to put out fires and have been equipped with the proper equipment, vehicles and instruments necessary to get to the fire and put it out! We must recognize that God has provided us with the training and equipment to rescue and put out those irritating, time consuming household "fires" that interrupt our day and get us off schedule. It's just another aspect of our many job descriptions.

For fire prevention, watch for behavioral changes and signs

of emotional "overloads". God designed us to bear one another's burden's (Galatians 6:2) and to cast all of our care upon Him (1 Peter 5:7). If we don't our emotions will squeal and signal spiritual alarms of approaching danger and fire damage. Be conscientious and aware of the fact that every day the enemy is stalking and seeking opportunity to sneak in unawares to strike a match of strife in a small corner of a room or brazenly throw a bomb of contention through your window to ignite fires. Examine yourself and make sure you're not the one playing with matches! I cannot tell you of the times I've awakened out of a bad dream and instead of praying; have given in to fear and watched before my very eyes the peace of my house be consumed by my emotional flames. I would continue to fuel the fire with agitation by entertaining the things I didn't get done the day before, and the proverbial question "why can't I get any help around here?"

Yes! There I was armed and ready to burn up everything in sight, but God in His mercy supplied the grace of His Word, which permeated and quenched roaring and out of control emotions with the assurance of His Sovereignty and that every thing round about me was under His control. This truth alone provides irrigating flood waters that transform dry, parched, desert-like circumstances into flowing reservoirs of peace.

You don't have to be susceptible to these kinds of self-destructive emotional outbursts. Before you go to bed and before you get up make sure that you saturate yourself in prayer. Prayer will drown internally unhealthy predatory thoughts and emotions that would, if allowed, try to overtake our confidence in God and destroy the peace He has provided for our home. Pray for

> Prayer will drown internally unhealthy predatory thoughts and emotions that would, if allowed, try to overtake our confidence in God and destroy the peace He has provided for our home.

your husband, pray for your family, pray for leadership, pray for every situation and circumstance that concerns you. Pray for yourself, pray for right thoughts; pray for forgiveness of sins and ask God to help you to do and say the right things. Romans 6:16 says,

> *Know ye not, that to whom ye yield yourselves servants to obey, his servants ye are to whom ye obey; whether of sin unto death, or of obedience unto righteousness?*

Your focus will determine your actions. If you submit to your thoughts and emotions you will find yourself a servant to chaos which is not an option. If we intend to be the recipients of right decisions, we must determine in our hearts to yield our will to the Holy Ghost and seek Godly wisdom for daily instructions.

Although it is human nature to trust in your own wisdom, we must be convinced that human wisdom is limited. The Bible says that earthly wisdom:

> *. . . descendeth not from above, but is earthly, sensual, devilish"* (James 3:15).

You can't accomplish every thing God wants you to accomplish with menial, moral senses oriented and demonically influenced wisdom. You need the power of the Holy Ghost leading and guiding you into all truth, (John 16:13) to destroy the barriers of deception and release you to hear and access the unlimited wealth and knowledge of God. Make the exchange, go to God, and prefer His way over your way, for a Spirit controlled life lends itself to peace and power with God!

FIVE

The Deception: "No One Cares About My Needs"

But my God shall supply all your need according to his riches in glory by Christ Jesus (Philippians 4:19).

 I'm reminded of the hymn "God Will Take Care of You", and my favorite verse:

Be not dismayed, whatever betide, God will take care of you, beneath his wings of love abide, God will take care of you.

This hymn to me depicts the paternal nature of God to provide for His children. It is who He is and what He does. God has made promises to "supply all our need", and is very aware of what you "have need of" (Matthew 6:32). He says your need is singular and not plural, and does not require that He perform an exhaustive amount of activity to take care of it. One Word from God can change your situation; one Word from God can provide you with all the peace, love, joy and sustenance you require.

We must realize that we are designed to rely on God (Proverbs 3:5),

> It is your Fathers good pleasure to give you the
> kingdom (Luke 12:32).

He wants to give you directions for getting your needs and answered prayers out of the heavens and into manifestation on earth.

Western civilization on the other hand thrives upon self-sufficiency, anxiety and stress. We live in a society that wants answers and resolutions quick, fast and in a hurry. We make our decisions on what we can see and feel. Believers must make a conscious decision not to be confined to limitations but gravitate to what the Word of God says about who we are and the unlimited power to which we have access, through our Lord and Savior Jesus Christ. God is provident; He has made provision for all our past, current and future needs. If you don't believe me, ask Him! He will tell you Himself!

SIX

The Deception: "I Can't Get No Satisfaction"

Let your conversation be without covetousness; and be content with such things as ye have: for he hath said, I will never leave thee, nor forsake thee. So that we may boldly say, The Lord is my helper, and I will not fear what man shall do unto me (Hebrews 13:5–6).

 Dissatisfaction leads to desperation. We find ourselves anxious over things we desire that we have not yet obtained. The Bible tells us in Proverbs 27:20:

Hell and destruction are never full; so the eyes of man are never satisfied.

The sooner we recognize this concept, the better off we will be. The will of man is constantly influenced by this world system that believes the more you have the better off you will be.

This appetite cultivates a vicious cycle. It is said that in our brain there is a pleasure center that it is stimulated by all kinds of pleasure; it craves to be stimulated and its goal is to be satisfied. Unfortunately, the problem with this pleasure center is the more it is stimulated, the more it takes to be stimulated. For example, if you stimulate your pleasure center by eating, it will require that you eat more and eventually become an overeater just to maintain that same level of stimulation. This is the birth of an addiction.

Our appetites crave sensual stimulation; see it, smell it, taste it, touch it or hear it, this is the constant battle between the flesh and the spirit. The flesh wants preeminence and to usurp its authority over the will of God.

In order for your spirit to win, you must fight the good fight of faith (1 Timothy 6:12) with the Word of God. Be mindful that unsatisfied flesh and a neglected relationship with Jesus Christ can only equate to taking matters into your own hands, causing desperate thinking, behavior and results.

Trying to satisfy the flesh develops into a entitlement mentality, an "I want it because I deserve it and if I have to, I'll take it". The book of James 4:5 in the Bible tells us the "Flesh lusteth to envy". It's not deep, it's just human nature in control, and as born again believers our Spirit is to war against that nature, bring it under subjection and be controlled by the Holy Ghost (Matthew 6:10).

> *This I say then, Walk in the Spirit, and ye shall not fulfill the lust of the flesh. For the flesh lusteth against the Spirit, and the Spirit against the flesh: and these are contrary the one to the other: so that ye cannot do the things that ye would* (Galatians 5:16, 17).

Walking in the Spirit requires regeneration and a desire to think and be like Christ (Philippians2:5). We can be like Christ, when we have His Spirit dwelling on the inside influencing us to do things His way. John 3:30 tells us:

He must increase, I must decrease.

Christ's agenda was to please the Father and our agenda is to please the Father by submitting and seeking His complete purpose and direction for our lives.

Thy kingdom come, Thy will be done on earth,
(in me,) as it is in heaven (Matthew 6:10).

It is humanly impossible to be desperate and led by the Spirit, for the Bible says in Isaiah 26:3:

Thou wilt keep him in perfect peace, whose mind
is stayed on thee: because he trusteth in thee.

We must allow the Word of God to focus our perspective, and not our or the opinion of others. Representing Christ requires that we operate with integrity and " . . . *be holy and without blame before him in love:*" (Ephesians 1:4). When we align ourselves with the Word of God, He reveals to us our true motives and why we may feel dissatisfied. We need to be truthful about how important appearances are to us and what we may consciously or unconsciously be doing to influence the opinions of others.

> Your flesh is never satisfied. This means you and all the other flesh around you.

As previously stated, your flesh is never satisfied. This means you and all the other flesh around you. God is the God of peace for your future and the here and now! Silence that flesh with the Word of God and rest in Him. Titus 1:15 tells us:

> *Unto the pure all things are pure: but unto them*
> *that are defiled and unbelieving is nothing pure;*
> *but even their mind and conscience is defiled.*

There is no way to influence someone to think positively about you if they are committed to impure thoughts of you. God is your helper; all rewards are of His doing, this is what you want to be satisfied with, not the temporal accolades of man. Don't be an approval seeker; this is an open gate to dissatisfaction. Obedience to God provides spiritual satisfaction that silences human cravings and the self motivated desires of immediate gratification. Don't allow any person, place or thing to rob you of the satisfying power of the Word of God.

SEVEN

The Deception:
"I'm Overwhelmed"

I can do all things through Christ which strengtheneth me (Philippians 4:13)

Most Christian women have been groomed to be the embodiment of the Proverbs 31 virtuous woman. Such aspirations are noble and to be diligently sought after within the confines of balance and contaminant free from self-righteousness works.

Philippians 4:13, a favorite scripture often quoted and more often misappropriated, is a plumb line for operating in balance. We tend to focus on the "I can do all things" without applying and experiencing the "through Christ which strengtheneth me". Trust me when I tell you that I speak from experience. Having 4 children, 5 years and under, I soon learned that you can only accomplish what God wants you to accomplish in the order He has instructed you to accomplish it! I remember one day I was doing the laundry, cleaning the kitchen and cooking dinner all at the same time. Things were going great. I was on schedule and things were getting checked off the checklist. As I began to fry the chicken chaos interrupted! The kids one by one began to come into the kitchen and decide that it was their turn to be an only child. I looked at the chicken frying in the hot oil and looked and listened to the kids graduate to a major uproar. What was I supposed to do? I casually ask God, "What is going on? Should I yell? Should I spank? Should I separate? What? Thank God for immediate answers. I took the chicken out of the oil, turned the frying pan off, and the kids ages 2, 3, 5 and 7 and I had a gospel music soul train line for 15 minutes. They soon settled down and watched T.V. and I finished dinner. They felt better and I felt better. I even out danced them all! I was not frustrated about being off schedule and I made a life time memory with the kids.

Neglecting your devotions will get you off track and send you into a flurry of activity that causes a downward spiral of fatigue and exhaustion which is all the wedge the enemy needs to launch his threats and accusations of defeatism.

I have learned that the only way to have real peace as a Christian housewife is to make it a habit to ask God for guidance before, during and after family calamities which seem to pop out of nowhere. It is the strategy of the enemy to cause us to be overwhelmed by our daily tasks. Divine direction from God will minimize and eliminate these feelings as we grow in grace and cause us to be victorious and triumphant instead of frustrated and overwhelmed.

Use wisdom; be led by the Holy Ghost, because without it success will cause you to do more than what God has asked you to do. Read, believe, practice and obey the Word of God. Neglecting your devotions will get you off track and send you into a flurry of activity that causes a downward spiral of fatigue and exhaustion which is all the wedge the enemy needs to launch his threats and accusations of defeatism.

Being overwhelmed by our circumstance will cause us to think and be tempted to sometimes speak, wrong thoughts like, "I don't have any help" or "I'm in this all by myself", similar to the prophet Elijah after the "Big Showdown on Mount Carmel".

The 450 prophets of Baal had their turn and now it was Elijah's. The Fire of the Lord fell, consumed the sacrifice and Baal prophets were destroyed. Elijah told Ahab to get ready for the great rain, and it did rain!

Now notice what the Bible says in I King 18:46:

> And the hand of the LORD was on Elijah; and
> he girded up his loins, and ran before Ahab to
> the entrance of Jezreel.

The power of God hit Elijah and he took off running in the rain and out ran Ahab's chariot. That victory had Elisha pumped and on fire and He took off running without instructions. Ahab goes and tells his wife Jezebel all that Elijah had done; Jezebel sends word to Elijah that she was going to have him killed by this time tomorrow and the next thing you know Elijah was on the run again.

Elijah ran for his life this time, running from Jezreel to Beersheba and then running "another day's journey". How many of you know that all that running is enough to wear an anointed prophet completely out! Elijah ran past his instruction and smack dab into the threat of death, fear of isolation and defeat until he collapsed from exhaustion and asked God to just kill him and get it over with.

Take a Nap, and Get Something to Eat

God was not impressed with Elijah's attitude of defeat; what else can you feel when you get off track. God allows Elijah to rest and go to sleep. The Angel of the Lord wakes him up, feeds him and lets him go back to sleep, wakes him up, feeds him again and lets him go back to sleep. God made provision for Elijah to eat and rest so he could have the stamina needed for the journey to hear from God. What a practical solution, food and rest for the body in preparation for the mental and physical endurance needed to get back on track so you can hear from God.

Nutrition and adequate rest are necessary components in combating fatigue, exhaustion and restoring mental and physical health. We need to keep in consideration that feelings of anxiety are sure indicators of fatigue and exhaustion. Make a habit of taking care of your temple of the Holy Ghost (I Corinthians 6:19).

Back on Track

After a forty day journey Elijah arrives at Mount Horeb. God causes a strong wind, earthquake and a fire. At the entrance of the cave, Elijah wraps his face with his mantle and hears God asks in a still small voice "What is your problem, Elijah?" God has Elijah's attention and begins to instruct Elijah (I King 19:13–19). Anoint Hazael to be king over Syria, Jehu king over Israel and Elisha to succeed you as prophet, and as an added footnote, don't be tricked! There are seven thousand in Israel that have not "kissed nor bowed".

God had answers and solutions all along for Elijah, but before Elijah could receive further instructions, he had to be in a place where he could hear God's voice. Like Elijah, if we allow a current victory to substitute further instruction from God, we will find ourselves in unguided activities, drained physically, mentally and spiritually. So remember, the next time you feel anxious, overwhelmed and consumed by fear of defeat, take a self-check and remember that the lack of God's instruction will cause you to be running on adrenalin alone and operating at a spiritual and physical deficit.

EIGHT

The Deception: "I'm Unfulfilled"

And now, brethren, I commend you to God, and to the word of his grace, which is able to build you up, and to give you an inheritance among all them which are sanctified (Acts 20:32).

Looking for meaning outside of motherhood, I began to seek external answers, in which I received a lot of information which left me even more confused and disgruntled. The women at church said I should be happy. I was married to a good man with a good job, I had children so I didn't have to worry about the ticking clock syndrome. You know the one; the single Christian woman's most dreaded time piece, "her biological clock".

On the other hand my professional friends seem to gravitate to inferences to my over contribution to population, I had 4 children and the national average was 2.5. They would continue their rhetoric with how significant professional working women are to their community, women causes and everything else that is important in the world. By the time they had finished with me I felt as though I had majored in and over-dosed on failure. And if that wasn't enough, I had to listen to further criticisms from teachers who would tell me I needed to spend more time with this child and relatives who would re-tort, "Don't be having all those babies on your husband", and last but not least, the housekeeping criticisms that varied from "if you want to keep your man happy" to "if you want your son not to have allergic reactions" then you better, . . . Wow! What a head trip!

Looking for entertainment therapy, I would turn on TV only to find myself bombarded with commercials which further attacked my self image. Thank God for His omnipresence. He saw me, preserved, consoled and restored me. He was right there observing it all and with perfect timing gave me what I needed when I needed it the most. God, my hero rescued me again from me.

I soon learned that we cannot buy into society's standards of fulfillment. This world system will have you entrenched in professional achievements and philanthropic causes, which when combined will still leave you unfulfilled. Fulfillment comes from seeking and doing the will of the Father. When you are outside of God's will, the most you can experience is imme-diate gratification and temporary gain. Doing God's will is what affords us the privilege of experiencing God's best for our lives. Total fulfillment only comes from being filled with the Spirit; if you find yourself half-filled drive into God's filling station and let the fuel of praise flow and "top off" your spiritual tank.

> *Wherefore be ye not unwise, but understanding what the will of the Lord is . . . but be filled with the Spirit; Speaking to yourselves in Psalm and hymns and spiritual songs, singing and making melody in your heart to the Lord;* (Ephesians 5:17–19).

NINE

The Deception: "I'm Lonely"

If ye abide in me, and my words abide in you, ye shall ask what ye will, and it shall be done unto you (John 15:7).

Your children are always around; breakfast, lunch and dinner, you run to the grocery store, church, PTA, soccer, and piano lessons. You have no real time for yourself, but yet you feel so alone. I, and a million other mothers, can relate. This is not a figment of your imagination, this situation is real, and the only solution is God.

God knows all we really need is some attention from Him. We need Him to take us to a place where we can nestle in and find refuge, a secret place in God where if needed we can linger and find a place of shelter that would become not only a location, but a residence. For this need is for more than mere social companionship, it is a need for spiritual therapy that only comes from worshipping the one and only, true and living God.

God brought me out of my place of loneliness, drew me

close and whispered gently, "Abide in me, for I am what you need."

I must confess He was absolutely right! I needed the all powerful God to soothe my thoughts, calm my fears and convince me that He had everything under control, and He did. And as an added bonus, God caused me to grow and love Him the more for it. I promise you, He has done this on several occasions for me, and if He did it for me, He will do it for you.

God loves and patiently waits for us. Jeremiah 31:3 says it like this:

> . . . *Yea, I have loved thee with an everlasting love: therefore with loving-kindness have I drawn thee.*

Wow! Take a minute and meditate on this scripture. He wants you to know that His love for you won't end, that it is everlasting and will not allow Him to become frustrated with you.

Your stubbornness does not aggravate God. He knows the when, where, what, why and how of your trepidation, and He has used your feelings of loneliness to get your attention, so you can get the attention you really need.

We tend to ignore the fact that God is a jealous God. Exodus 34:14 says it plainly:

> *For thou shalt worship no other god: for the LORD, whose name is Jealous, is a jealous God.*

God does not play; He does not want anything or anyone to take His place. God wants us to be devoted to Him. Oftentimes we make the mistake of giving preeminence and priority to things that monopolize our time and attention. God's not havin' it! We normally can detect when spouses or children are jealous; behaviors change, responses change and attitudes change. Likewise, if things that normally give you contentment leave you feeling lonely and unfulfilled and if normal life responses seem askew, it's probably a good sign that life has revolted and aligned itself in agreement with the jealousy God has for you.

God is in love with you, God is Jealous for you; don't settle for the emotional insecurity of loneliness, run into the arms of God and be consumed by the power of His presence.

Maintain a heightened sense of awareness of your spiritual advancement into the kingdom of God. Revelation is double sided. Luke 12:48b tells us:

> *. . . if normal life responses seem askew, it's probably a good sign that life has revolted and aligned itself in agreement with the jealousy God has for you.*

> *For unto whomsoever much is given, of him shall be much required:*

Spending more time with God will disperse feelings of loneliness and grant you revelation of who He is and what He wants from you. More revelation means more truth; more truth requires a greater commitment to maintain and spread the truth. The light of revelation dispels the darkness of deception. Stay connected to Jesus and He will void the dark places of loneliness and fill them with the light of His Love.

TEN

The Deception: "I'm Depressed"

Casting all your care upon him; for he careth for you (1 Peter 5:7).

This scripture is the perfect weapon for casting down thoughts that lead to depression. The enemy will accuse you with thoughts of isolation and abandonment. He's a liar! God cares about everything that you go through. He's available to express the love, comfort and provision for your every need. You must believe God when He says in Hebrew 13:5

. . . I will never leave thee, nor forsake thee.

Even when it seems that God is not there, anchor yourself in His promise and realize this is a predetermined exercise for your faith. Look past the physical evidence that's trying to dictate itself above God's truth, overlook your current emotional state and focus on your training exercise. I'm sure you can relate to the word *exercise*. At some point and time most of us have made a decision to allot a certain amount of time in our schedule to exercise; and for those of us who were not committed to this decision it became a burden. For those of us who persevered, we were rewarded with weight loss, added energy and stamina. The difference between the two opinions are the one focused on how uncomfortable it would be and how difficult it was to fit into an already time slot filled day. The other perspective recognized the necessity of remaining focused to attain the end result.

Exercise the enemy's lies away by lifting the Word of God to its rightful place in your life.

Encourage Yourself

Wanting to feel the care and concern of others is very natural, but in the event that you don't receive it, don't allow it to elevate the "no one cares" platform. God has people praying for you that you may not be aware of, so press beyond feelings of rejection and encourage yourself. I promise you it is a good thing to practice. The more you practice encouraging yourself the less encouragement you will need from others.

The enemy fights to make you feel as though God does not care. He brings thoughts like "If God cared so much, why is He allowing this to happen?" You should respond as if a stranger is trying to get in your personal business, and say "Get out my face, This ain't your business!"

> Learn to tell the enemy he has no right to talk to you, let alone ask you a question!

Learn to tell the enemy he has no right to talk to you, let alone ask you a question! His authority is permanently revoked. Every time he tries to lure you away from God's Word with lies, respond like Jesus and immediately use the truth of God's Word to put the devil in his powerless place.

Read and memorize the Word of God, this will give you the tools to cast down every negative emotion with the Word of God. Fill your day with opportunities to hear and see scriptures. The Word of God is alive and it will flow into every willing heart and soul when given opportunity and its life giving properties will be a source of companionship and comfort and reaffirm that you are never alone.

ELEVEN

Mission Accomplished: The Accuser Identified!

> *And I heard a loud voice saying in heaven, Now is come salvation, and strength, and the kingdom of our God, and the power of his Christ: for the accuser of our brethren is cast down, which accused them before our God day and night* (Revelation 12:10).

We could go on an on about the enemy's countless accusations to convict us with guilt for past faults and deceptive lies about the people we love to indict us in unforgiveness. The mission has been accomplished. We can be confident that his tactics have been exposed; he is after our faith, he wants us to trust his deception and not have faith in God's Word. We now know how to recognize and reject every form of deceptive tactics. James 4:7 instructs us to:

> *Submit yourselves therefore to God. Resist the devil, and he will flee from you.*

You cannot be successful in resisting the devil, until you submit unto God and you must do it in that exact order.

So whenever situations seems to dictate feelings of isolation, anxiety and being overwhelmed, immediately cast them down and exalt the knowledge of God, (2 Corinthians 2:5) and focus in on the grace Christ has given you for your life.

God's image of you

If you still struggle with failures, short comings and weaknesses, you undoubtedly need your confidence built up in the promises of God. Seek God earnestly, pour out your heart and be determined that you will not allow the discomfort of your flesh to supersede the provision for peace in the knowledge of the sovereignty of God.

Pray His Word! It is alive, it is powerful, and it will discern the author and intent of your every thought (Hebrew 4:12). Remember, you are not powerless, and you are not alone! God is on your side. Romans 8:31 tells us:

> *What shall we then say to these things? If God*
> *be for us, who can be against us?*

Make a decision to be influential and not influenced by the inundation of doubt and negativity of this world system. You have mountain moving ability (Matthew 21:21); get this revelation and make it experiential, practice it, apply it, be motivated by it, use it and by all means, share it. Romans 10:8, 9 is applicable to the salvation of your soul from sin, sickness, disease and poverty. It reads:

> *But what saith it? The word is nigh thee, even*
> *in thy mouth, and in thy heart: that is, the word*
> *of faith, which we preach; That if thou shalt*

confess with thy mouth the Lord Jesus, and shalt believe in thine heart that God hath raised him from the dead, thou shalt be saved,

God is in the saving business; His kingdom has come to save you from being a victim of the fallen nature of sin. The Holy Ghost gives faith to believe in God's Word to change you from mortal to immortality, sickness to divine health and lack to posterity. Get this Word and spread it!

There are souls to be saved, wounds to be healed, bondages to be destroyed, and hearts to be mended. The more you use it, the more it will work for you. Declare God's deliverance to everyone you know, that the Word of God is able to make you free. Make up in your mind that this is what you are called to do.

God's Image for your Home

Oftentimes we have the wrong conceptions of spiritual warfare. The enemy has been defeated; our fight is within our flesh to maintain our faith. Take a spiritual inventory of your home, start with you, make sure activities align themselves with the Word of God.

We seem to be more astute in the need for deliverance of those outside of our home; we can identify the drunk on the corner, the homosexual at the hairdressers and the adulteress neighbor, that's pretty obvious to us. But when it comes to isolating the strongholds and spirits in our children we tend to generalize them away as phases. We can look at our spouses and name them as the single most cause of our frustration. We can find occasions to expose what we feel is their ineptness and see so much in everyone else, but we can't seem to see the enemy reeking havoc through us in our home. Now if that ain't warfare, I don't know what is!

But that's over now! It's time to change our posture girls, and see things as they really are. We have been anointed to identify the enemy's deceptive strategies in the spirit and to cover those we love, not fight in the flesh and expose their faults and weaknesses.

There may be days when your judgment is clouded and you find yourself asking the question "What is really goin' on?" I tell you what the Bible says is really goin' on! Ephesians 6:12 tells us:

> *For we wrestle not against flesh and blood, but against principalities, against powers, against the rulers of the darkness of this world, against spiritual wickedness in high places.*

This scripture lets us know exactly what we are up against, which is an organized demonic hierarchy trying to regain authority. We know the truth; he is defeated, the mental games of deception are no power against the Word of God. He can't force his way in, nor trick us into letting him in, for the Holy Ghost is our intrusion detection system. Keep your house free from invasions, be proactive and not reactive. Read the Word of God and keep it fresh in your mind, look for opportunities to apply the Word of God. Look for Jesus in every situation, ask Him, "God where are you in all of this, what do you want me to do, and what do you want me to say?" Seek Jesus for guidance; remind Him of His Word and your desire to obey it and pray:

> *God, I don't want to get involved in anything you don't want me involved in, don't let me feel anything you don't want me to feel, and don't allow me to get caught up or excited about anything you're not in!!!*

Ladies, this means war, constant war and you have already been declared the winner. Get your gear and let's go to battle! If there has been a lodged attack against your home, it is high time for YOU to fight back!

It is time to make a declaration:

We ain't goin' out like that!

You can't have my husband!
You can't have my children!
You can't have my home!
You can't have my physical or mental health!
You can't have my prosperity!
You can't have me!

Paul says it best in Romans 8:37–39:

> *Nay, in all these things we are more than conquerors through him that loved us. For I am persuaded, that neither death, nor life, nor angels, nor principalities, nor powers, nor things present, nor things to come, Nor height, nor depth, nor any other creature, shall be able to separate us from the love of God, which is in Christ Jesus our Lord.*

Stand on God's Word and maintain your position!

RECIPES

I AM NOT A DESPERATE HOUSEWIFE

Mix It With Faith!

For unto us was the gospel preached, as well as unto them: but the word preached did not profit them, not being mixed with faith in them that heard it (Hebrews 4:2).

In the profound words of my pastor, Marvin Winans, you have to "Get this Word down in your belly!" You can't just read it, write it, quote it and memorize it, you have to believe and experience it. You must believe even when your situation stands diametrically opposed to the Word of God.

When your marriage seems to be failing, when your kids are trying to go astray and when yielding to temptation seems like your only way out, use the passage of scripture that opposes your situation and choose to be confident in the "substance" and "evidence" of the faith in the Word of God (Hebrews 11:1). Faith will cause a metamorphosis of a perceived failure into *"more than a conqueror"* (Romans 8:37).

Mixing the Word of God with faith creates spiritual combustion that detonates and explodes the facts and deception of this world's system, and releases the manifested power and experiential knowledge of God into your life.

Prosperity

> *Blessed is the man that walketh not in the counsel of the ungodly, nor standeth in the way of sinners, nor sitteth in the seat of the scornful. But his delight is in the law of the LORD; and in his law doth he meditate day and night. And he shall be like a tree planted by the rivers of water, that bringeth forth his fruit in his season; his leaf also shall not wither; and whatsoever he doeth shall prosper* (Psalm 1:1–3).

This is incredible; God starts the Book of Psalms with instructions for prosperity. This should convince you that God wants you to be prosperous. What kind of father would allow his children to be destitute? Not yours! Reflect on the city of heaven, foundation walls made of precious stones, streets of gold and pearl gates (Revelations 21:18–21). Our Lord Jesus Christ has unlimited ability and resources. Align your life with His Word and you will prosper in whatever you do!

God's Presence

Who shall ascend into the hill of the LORD? Or who shall stand in his holy place? He that hath clean hands, and a pure heart; who hath not lifted up his soul unto vanity, nor sworn deceitfully. He shall receive the blessing from the LORD, and righteousness from the God of his salvation (Psalm 24:1–5).

God is Holy, and His presence requires purity, humility and truth. You may feel that this is hard to achieve, when in fact it is really quite simple. All it takes is repentance. Repentance releases the shed blood of Christ, the sin cleansing agent that leaves you "clean" by faith "with the washing of water by the word," (Ephesians 5:26).

Don't allow the guilt of sin to exclude you from God's presence. You have a forgiving God, waiting to give audience to the petitions of His child. He's waiting for you and holding your seat, hurry up and get there.

Good, Long, Life

> *What man is he that desireth life, and loveth many days, that he may see good? Keep thy tongue from evil, and thy lips from speaking guile. Depart from evil, and do good; seek peace, and pursue it* (Psalm 34:12–14).

You read it right! This is a detailed recipe for those who want to experience some good things and live a long life: shut your mouth, don't be sneaky, do good things and be a proactive peacemaker.

Observe this Word with faith and watch God act upon it. Jeremiah 1:12 tells us that God watches "over his word to perform it". Give God something to look at, exhibit this Word so He can reward you with a good, long, life!

Encouragement

Why art thou cast down, O my soul? and why art thou disquieted in me? Hope thou in God: for I shall yet praise him for the help of his countenance (Psalm 42:5).

This scripture lets us know that there may be times when you experience some discouraging situations. Don't let these circumstances and your limited ability make you worry. "How do I not worry?" you may ask, "How do I start a praise fest or choose to praise God instead?" I dare you to say with conviction "Hallelujah, Thank you Jesus, You are greater than my problem, I don't *accept* worry, but I do give you the PRAISE!"

WARNING:

This type of praise when done sincerely causes exhilaration and may provoke an immediate response from God. You may be thrust into His presence; make sure you have on comfortable clothing, and try not to drive or operate heavy machinery.

Security

> *He that dwelleth in the secret place of the most*
> *High shall abide under the shadow of the Almighty.*
> *I will say of the LORD, He is my refuge and my*
> *fortress: my God; in him will I trust* (Psalm 91:1–2).

We live in a society which capitalizes on our affinity for fear. Television news broadcasts crime and their victims, our newspapers mimic its headlines with pages filled with panic of war, death, famine and disease. We are saturated with stories about gas prices and unemployment on the increase, wages and health benefits on the decline. Mixed in between the lines and pages are security device advertisements camouflaging as the solution. We purchase them in the hope of feeling safe, only to see in next month's headline how crafty criminals have made them obsolete.

This world system thrives upon creating chaos to implement its solution. Don't buy into the hype; Andre Crouch eloquently sings it best in this lyric:

> *Jesus is the answer for the world today, above Him*
> *there's no other. Jesus is the way.*

We have been given the only fool proof security system for life, and that is the safety of a living and loving relationship with God.

Don't allow the insecurities of life to motivate you to take matters into your own hands and move outside the security of God's Word. There is no safety outside of His will, stay under the superiority and omnipotence of His Word, for His "covering" provides a strong, secured place of refuge for safe living in chaotic surroundings.

Reasons to Praise

Make a joyful noise unto the LORD, all ye lands. Serve the LORD with gladness: come before his presence with singing. Know ye that the LORD he is God: it is he that hath made us, and not we ourselves; we are his people, and the sheep of his pasture. Enter into his gates with thanksgiving, and into his courts with praise: be thankful unto him, and bless his name. For the LORD is good; his mercy is everlasting; and his truth endureth to all generations (Psalm 100:1–5).

Praise activates Faith. Faith directs the hand of God. The more we sing, dance and celebrate the power of God's Word over the fear of our circumstance, the more we realize God's eternal goodness, mercy and truth.

Praise God for who He is, Praise Him for what He does, find a way to praise God in your most difficult circumstance and it will lead you to a pasture of provision and comfort.

Purposeful Life

I shall not die, but live, and declare the works of the LORD (Psalm 118:17).

God gives us purpose. No matter who you are, your obligation as a believer is to spread the gospel. Live the life and be *"known and read of all men"* (2 Corinthians 3:2). You have a testimony that someone needs to hear, so they too can be inspired to "live and not die". Purpose in your heart to tell people that it is God's goodness that sustains, motivates and blesses you. Telling God's goodness is transmittable, the more you tell, the more you will encourage others to tell. This will motivate believers and unbelievers to get what you have so they too can "declare the works of the LORD!"

Sin Resistance

> *Thy word have I hid in mine heart, that I might not sin against thee* (Psalm 119:11).

The Bible says *"Good understanding giveth favour: but the way of transgressors is hard."* (Proverbs 13:15). If you are in a constant struggle with that same old sin, ask God to show you what is the real root of the problem, and ask Him to show you how to allow His Word to comfort you instead of the immediate gratification of that sin. Listen for direction, God has answers for you in His Word. Don't allow temptation to overwhelm you! I Corinthians 10:13 encourages:

> *There hath no temptation taken you but such as is common to man: but God is faithful, who will not suffer you to be tempted above that ye are able; but will with the temptation also make a way to escape, that ye may be able to bear it.*

The Word of God is provided for you so that you will be able to counter attack your sin temptation.

Commit scripture to memory and don't look at sin's temptation as an opportunity to fail, look at it as an opportunity to experience and use the power of God's Word living in you. In the eloquent words of our Pastor, Pastor Marvin L. Winans:

> *It will work, if you work it.*

Total Commitment

*Teach me, O LORD, the way of thy statutes; and I
shall keep it unto the end. Give me understanding,
and I shall keep thy law; yea, I shall observe it with
my whole heart* (Psalm 119:33–34).

God has given us His Spirit to help teach us the power of His
Word. The love for God and the power of His Word in our
lives develops our commitment to God. The Holy Ghost reveals the exact meaning and intent for daily application in your
life.

The Holy Ghost is given to us to dwell in us as a constant
beacon to navigate through God's Word. John 14:26 tells us:

*But the Comforter, which is the Holy Ghost, whom
the Father will send in my name, he shall teach you
all things, and bring all things to your remembrance, whatsoever I have said unto you.*

In order to have the Word of God in daily operation in
your life, you need the power of the Holy Ghost. The Holy
Ghost makes the Word of God alive, tangible and obtainable.
It is the catalyst that drives our commitment to God. It is God's
Spirit in us working "*both to will and to do*" (Philippians
2:13). The Holy Ghost teaches and gives the revelation which
compels you to be "Totally Committed".

Clarity

Thy word is a lamp unto my feet, and a light unto my path (Psalm 119:105).

So much to do, and so little time, the cares of life have a way of making it difficult to decipher the path to travel. Everyone has an idea or an opinion on how you should get to where God has told you to go. Don't be seduced by the lights and speed of the highways of life, follow the road least traveled. Matthew 7:13, 14 reads:

> *Enter ye in at the strait gate: for wide is the gate, and broad is the way, that leadeth to destruction, and many there be which go in thereat: Because strait is the gate, and narrow is the way, which leadeth unto life, and few there be that find it.*

God has a specific word, for every decision or step that you make. Don't be in a hurry, seek God out through His Word and He will give illumination to avoid the traffic jam of confusion and see clearly the road specifically designed to get you to your destiny.

Confidence

Thou art my hiding place and my shield: I hope in thy word (Psalm 119:114).

Confidence in the Word of God gives you a place to resort in time of trouble. Life's dictates will move you to fear and make you run for shelter outside of the Word of God. Decide to trust God's Word; that trust will envelope you and create a fortress, a hiding place and will shield you from the hazards of panic and fear.

Great Peace

*Great peace have they which love thy law: and
nothing shall offend them* (Psalm 119:165).

Offenses are like heat seeking missiles being guided by those
"hot spot" targets in our emotions. These offenses are
launched to mortally wound and destroy. The peace of God
acts as a "cooling agent", shielding us from the constant bomb
threats and makes us mobile "hard targets" impervious to the
snares and traps of the enemy. Great peace comes from a re-
solve to hold fast to and be governed by the Word of God.
Great peace is the result of loving and making God's Word
your life's priority.

Consolation

> *I will lift up mine eyes unto the hills, fro m whence cometh my help. My help cometh from the LORD, which made heaven and earth. He will not suffer thy foot to be moved: he that keepeth thee will not slumber. Behold, he that keepeth Israel shall neither slumber nor sleep. The LORD is thy keeper: the LORD is thy shade upon thy right hand. The sun shall not smite thee by day, nor the moon by night. The LORD shall preserve thee from all evil: he shall preserve thy soul. The LORD shall preserve thy going out and thy coming in from this time forth, and even for evermore* (Psalm121:1–8).

Consolation comes from positioning and receiving. You must assume the spiritual position in order to receive the Word that will bring you consolation. Your spiritual eyes must direct your mental focus. You must place more value toward God's promise of consolation and not the situation.

Tuning in to God's frequency will synchronize the broadcasted Word of God to your situation and cause you to hear and receive comfort from station B-I-B-L-E, the best station for receiving comfort from the God of consolation.

Reward of Tears

They that sow in tears shall reap in joy (Psalm 126:5).

Tears are seeds. Crying to God sows these seeds into His heart and will reap high yielding crops of joy. Faith in God's compassion is the good and fertile ground that brings forth this valuable fruit. This faith is not the result of limited cognitive understanding which is brought about by facts and reasoning. This understanding only comes from the assurance that God is involved and He hears, sees, knows, understands and is looking out for your best interest. Remember, hurt, pain and tears do not have the last say, they are part of a sowing process which ends in a harvest of unspeakable joy!

Assurance

The LORD will perfect that which concerneth me: thy mercy, O LORD, endureth for ever: forsake not the works of thine own hands (Psalm 138:8).

Being a housewife will automatically thrust you into the problem solving arena and part of being a successful problem solver will require that you first examine yourself to see what part you might have played in the problem. Always keep in mind that taking responsibility for your error is one thing, but being overly introspective and magnifying your areas of weakness is taking responsibility to the extreme.

God knows everything about you, trust Him; your weakness is not stronger than God. God created you, and He can and He will fix you. You are not too hard for God. He will fix you and all the things that concern you, from the greatest to the least. If it is important to you, it is important to God, He will not give up on you. You are an important investment to Him. Jeremiah 29:11–13 reads:

> *For I know the thoughts that I think toward you, saith the LORD, thoughts of peace, and not of evil, to give you an expected end. Then shall ye call upon me, and ye shall go and pray unto me, and I will hearken unto you. And ye shall seek me, and find me, when ye shall search for me with all your heart.*

Tell God your heart; He's waiting, He's wanting and He's willing to work out every quirk and perfect every gift.

Attentiveness

How precious also are thy thoughts unto me, O God! how great is the sum of them! If I should count them, they are more in number than the sand: when I awake, I am still with thee (Psalm 139:17–18).

We are motivated to make sure that every one in our family experiences something that makes them feel special. Unfortunately, we regularly find our selves a victim of our motivation, we're often unappreciated, ignored and taken for granted, but that's just the nature of our business as housewives.

God sees your every sacrifice, He sees your gentleness, your compassion and all those little things that you do that go unnoticed. He notices them and wants you to know that those are the things that He loves about you. You are always on His mind and He wants to tell you how special you are to Him and how much He loves you. God wants to spend some time talking to you about how much He appreciates you for being obedient and being used of Him to demonstrate His love toward your family. He appreciates the fact that He can depend on you to show His love. God is devoted to you and He thinks about you all the time and every time you wake up, He's right there waiting to give you the attention and motivation you need to do His will for the day.

Guarded Heart

> *Set a watch, O LORD, before my mouth; keep the door of my lips. Incline not my heart to any evil thing, to practise wicked works with men that work iniquity: and let me not eat of their dainties.* (Psalm 141:3–4).

In order to watch what comes out of your mouth, you have to watch what enters your heart. David says in Psalm 101:3:

> *I will set no wicked thing before mine eyes:*

You have to be mindful of everything you watch. You have to tell yourself "I can't look at that!" If it goes against the Word of God, you cannot allow it to enter into your heart, through your sight.

You cannot listen to just anything, you cannot laugh at just any thing, you cannot respond to just anything and you cannot hang around just anything. And whatever you do, make sure that you do not make friendships and alliances with those who do the things that God tells you not to do. Proverbs 23:7a instructs: *"For as he thinketh in his heart, so is he:"*

What you see, hear and surround yourself with influences your thought life.

Use the Word of God. It will act as a security device to monitor and guard against illegal evils.

Justice

Let the high praises of God be in their mouth, and a twoedged sword in their hand; To execute vengeance upon the heathen, and punishments upon the people; To bind their kings with chains, and their nobles with fetters of iron; To execute upon them the judgment written: this honour have all his saints. Praise ye the Lord (Psalm 149:6–9).

One of the greatest misnomers of Christendom is that saint's cain't fight. That's a lie! Yes, we can! This misconception has left many young Christians feeling powerless and frustrated. The wisdom of God teaches us to fight on our turf! We have to learn to take our fights out of the earthly realm and into the "spiritual streets!" On the spiritual streets, we are mighty through God and don't have to succumb to weapons of intimidation, threats, fists, feet, knives or guns. We have a more formidable weapon, which is exultation and the Word of God.

We speak it and God moves on it. So before and/or during any attack, keep swinging with exultation, for

> *. . . the kingdom of heaven suffereth violence, and the violent take it by force* (Matthew 11:12).

There has been an attack to prevent the people of God from doing things God's way. We cannot just sit back and allow the limitations of this world system to be shoved down our throats. "We ain't goin' out like that!" Force the issue and exalt the Word of God over and above,

> *. . . every high thing that exalteth itself against the knowledge of God . . .* (2 Corinthians 10:5).

The kingdoms of this world are become the kingdoms of our Lord, and of his Christ; and he shall reign for ever and ever (Revelation 11:15).

Don't settle for anything less. We can have it right here and right now! Matthew 6:10 teaches us to pray:

Thy kingdom come. Thy will be done in earth, as it is in heaven.

Praise Instructions

> *Praise ye the Lord. Praise God in his sanctuary: praise him in the firmament of his power. Praise him for his mighty acts: praise him according to his excellent greatness. Praise him with the sound of the trumpet: praise him with the psaltery and harp. Praise him with the timbrel and dance: praise him with stringed instruments and organs. Praise him upon the loud cymbals: praise him upon the high sounding cymbals. Let every thing that hath breath praise the Lord. Praise ye the Lord (Psalm 150:1–6).*

God's Book of Psalms is climaxed with instructions in reference to the who, what, when, where, and how of praise. This scripture instructs us:

> Because of **Who** He is, Praise HIM!.
> Because of **What** He's done, Praise HIM!
> **When** you're in Church, Praise HIM!
> **When** you see and feel His power, stop and give HIM some Praise! Think about **How** great He is! That's right, give HIM some more Praise!

While you're praising make sure His praise is equivalent to His sovereignty. If you can play an instrument, Praise HIM on that! Get your whole body involved, move your hands and your feet, get loud with it, and last but not least, if you think that your past sin prevents your obligation or worthiness to praise, think again and remember the bottom line is this, the ending phrase of the Psalm. If you have breath, you are mandated to give God HIS Praise! He made you His praise, now you make Him yours!

Direction

Trust in the Lord with all thine heart; and lean not unto thine own understanding. In all thy ways acknowledge him, and he shall direct thy paths (Proverbs 3:5–6).

Trusting in the Lord with all your heart mandates that you relinquish your human perception to evaluate and rationalize your circumstantially based limited experience. Your automatic response must be to ask God "What is really going on?" Resorting to God's infinite power and ability makes us come to terms with how inadequate we are to assess a demonic influence cloaked in a physical manifestation on our own. We have to make pursuing God's understanding a constant desire. Vacillating back to your reasoning will leave you misplaced and off course. If you purpose in your heart to seek God in everything, you can be confident that He will lead you in the right direction.

Preservation

*Get wisdom, get understanding: forget it not; nei-
ther decline from the words of my mouth. Forsake
her not, and she shall preserve thee: love her, and
she shall keep thee. Wisdom is the principal thing;
therefore get wisdom: and with all thy getting get
understanding* (Proverbs 4:5–7).

The courses of life always present challenges. These challenges can seem to be life threatening, but they are no threat
to the wisdom of God. The wisdom of God will give you divine revelation on how to respond no matter how difficult the
circumstance. God will tell you what to say or what not to
say, what to do or what not to do and sometimes to just be
still. Make God's Word your life's sustenance, make a commitment to obey it and He will preserve you with wisdom
and understanding.

Perpetual Blessing

The blessing of the LORD, it maketh rich, and he addeth no sorrow with it (Proverbs 10:22).

There are times when it seems that what you once prayed for, received and deemed your blessing has now demonstrated burdensome characteristics. Sometimes it seems easier to receive a blessing from God than it is to maintain it. Always keep in mind that if it took faith to get it, it will take faith to keep it. The natural man cannot receive the spiritual things of God, so you must not rely on your natural ability alone to maintain the blessings of God. The nature of God's blessings yields increase, God will sustain what He ordains; do not pollute your blessing from God by trying to maintain or grow it on your own. Trust that what God gives requires you to stay in relationship with Him to maintain. Continue in Him, and He will continue to bless it and make it a continually increased harvest.

Generosity

The liberal soul shall be made fat: and he that watereth shall be watered also himself (Proverbs 11:25).

Generosity moves God. When you consistently meet that needs of others, it moves God to move in behalf of your need. God is a generous God, and when He sees Himself being manifested in His children, it compels Him to reward us from His unlimited supply of resources.

Profit

In all labour there is profit: but the talk of the lips tendeth only to penury (Proverbs 14:23).

Regardless of your ambitions, what you do will determine what you get back in return. Talking must be supported by hard work. Put an effort behind your conversation; just talking will only lead to lack.

God gives the necessary tools to prosper, don't just talk about it, do something with it!

Less Trouble

Whoso keepeth his mouth and his tongue keepeth his soul from troubles (Proverbs 21:23).

God gives us a very basic equation: talking too much equals added troubles. Not saying every thing that comes to your mind will keep you out of a lot of unnecessary drama. Make it a habit to limit yourself to only so many words, comments and conversations a day. You will be surprised at how your quality of life will improve!

Virtuous Woman

*Who can find a virtuous woman? for her price is far
above rubies. The heart of her husband doth safely
trust in her, so that he shall have no need of spoil.
She will do him good and not evil all the days of her
life. She seeketh wool, and flax, and worketh will-
ingly with her hands. She is like the merchants'
ships; she bringeth her food from afar. She riseth
also while it is yet night, and giveth meat to her
household, and a portion to her maidens. She con-
sidereth a field, and buyeth it: with the fruit of her
hands she planteth a vineyard. She girdeth her loins
with strength, and strengtheneth her arms. She per-
ceiveth that her merchandise is good: her candle
goeth not out by night. She layeth her hands to the
spindle, and her hands hold the distaff. She stretch-
eth out her hand to the poor; yea, she reacheth forth
her hands to the needy. She is not afraid of the snow
for her household: for all her household are clothed
with scarlet. She maketh herself coverings of tapes-
try; her clothing is silk and purple. Her husband is
known in the gates, when he sitteth among the elders of the land. She maketh fine linen, and selleth it;
and delivereth girdles unto the merchant. Strength
and honour are her clothing; and she shall rejoice in
time to come. She openeth her mouth with wisdom;
and in her tongue is the law of kindness. She
looketh well to the ways of her household, and
eateth not the bread of idleness. Her children arise
up, and call her blessed; her husband also, and he
praiseth her. Many daughters have done virtuously,*

but thou excellest them all. Favour is deceitful, and beauty is vain: but a woman that feareth the LORD, she shall be praised. Give her of the fruit of her hands; and let her own works praise her in the gates (Proverbs 31:10–3).

This passage of scripture is the lifestyle blue print to which to aspire. The key phrase here is life style. Be mindful that:

To every thing there is a season, and a time to every purpose under the heaven: (Ecclesiastes 3:1).

This virtuous woman had to check that field out before she bought it and planted during planting season. God wants us to lead a full and balanced life; He does not want you to get carried away with such lofty goals that leave you sick, broke, busted and disgusted. God may give you the big picture, but you still have to wait for His detailed instructions. Find yourself in this scripture or where you are supposed to be and work it until He tells you differently!

Provision

> *Ask, and it shall be given you; seek, and ye shall find; knock, and it shall be opened unto you: For every one that asketh receiveth; and he that seeketh findeth; and to him that knocketh it shall be opened* (Matthew 7:7–8).

God loves His children, and it is His nature to nurture and provide for them. As His children, we have a responsibility to maintain our relationship with Him. This relationship requires open, honest and constant communication. By praying, fasting and reading God's Word, we are taught His will, what to believe God for and how to live to please Him. Living in relationship builds expectation, an expectation that encourages you to "come boldly before the throne of grace" (Hebrews 4:16) and continually ask, seek and knock.

Luke 12:32 tells us:

> *Fear not, little flock; for it is your Father's good pleasure to give you the kingdom.*

Go to God for He has already made provision for everything you need; He is waiting for you to ask, seek and knock.

Rest

> Come unto me, all ye that labour and are heavy
> laden, and I will give you rest. Take my yoke upon
> you, and learn of me; for I am meek and lowly in
> heart: and ye shall find rest unto your souls
> For my yoke is easy, and my burden is light"
> (Matthew 11:28–30).

God has a supernatural exchange rate. In order to participate, you must be willing to relinquish what He asks of you so can get what He wants to give. He does not want you to struggle unnecessarily or try to figure out on your own things that are meant for Him to handle. Give your pain, frustration, insecurity and questions to Jesus, follow His instructions, do what He says so you can receive His freely given "righteousness and peace and joy in the Holy Ghost" (Romans 14:17).

Successful Prayers

Jesus answered and said unto them, Verily I say unto you, If ye have faith, and doubt not, ye shall not only do this which is done to the fig tree, but also if ye shall say unto this mountain, Be thou removed, and be thou cast into the sea; it shall be done. And all things, whatsoever ye shall ask in prayer, believing, ye shall receive (Matthew 21:21–22).

God wants us to believe everything He says He can do. We have a tendency to limit infinite God to our finite expectations. God is so much bigger than that! His Word teaches us time and time again of His awesome greatness and power. We need to settle this issue once and for all and believe when we pray that God is able to answer what may feel like the most difficult prayer.

If you need the impossible, believe for the impossible, pray and ask God to search and purify your motive for what you ask. For faith will only attach itself to pure motives. Successful prayers require successful asking. You need the Holy Ghost to tell you what to pray and the Word of God to remove doubt and secure the faith needed so you can receive your granted request. God is waiting, willing and able to do His part; allow God to purify your desires and you will receive the "whatever" you are asking for.

Things Revealed

For nothing is secret, that shall not be made manifest; neither any thing hid, that shall not be known and come abroad (Luke 8:1).

Have you ever lost something and you could not find it? Or have you ever had a circumstance that did not seem quite right, and the thought of it kept nudging at you? God has answers for your questions and direction for dealing with unsettling situations. Pray this scripture and if you have the Holy Ghost He will reveal to you what you need to know and how you should go about handling your every situation.

Authority

> *Behold, I give unto you power to tread on serpents and scorpions, and over all the power of the enemy: and nothing shall by any means hurt you* (Luke 10:19).

We do not have to subject ourselves to physical, mental and emotional threats; we have been given power sealed with a promise that nothing can hurt us. Take back and maintain your position of authority which is your right as a child of God. Do not succumb to threats of intimidation but plead the blood of Jesus instead. There is power in His Blood and it is the barrier of protection for the born again believer.

Believe and speak the power of God's Word, walk in it and never turn away from it again!

Purity

> *The light of the body is the eye: therefore when*
> *thine eye is single, thy whole body also is full of*
> *light; but when thine eye is evil, thy body also is full*
> *of darkness. Take heed therefore that the light*
> *which is in thee be not darkness. If thy whole body*
> *therefore be full of light, having no part dark, the*
> *whole shall be full of light, as when the bright shin-*
> *ing of a candle doth give thee light* (Luke
> 11:34–36).

It is so vitally important that as Christians we aggressively pursue maintaining our purity. We must cleanse ourselves from the
contaminants of this world and purge our hearts of subtle old
behaviors that try to creep back into our lives from before our
regeneration. We must cleanse ourselves daily "with the washing of water by the word," (Ephesians 5:26) and pray:

> *Create in me a clean heart, O God; and renew a*
> *right spirit within me* (Psalm 51:10).

A pure heart demands that we keep a spirit of repentance
and a desire to obey. If we do so God promises this benefit in
Matthew 5:8:

> *Blessed are the pure in heart: for they shall see God.*

Order

But rather seek ye the kingdom of God; and all
these things shall be added unto you (Luke 12:31).

Have you ever had so many things to do, only so much time to get them completed and you did not quite know where to start? Here's the solution. Devote time first thing in the morning to God; ask Him how He would have you spend your day.

The Kingdom of God consists of order and you are part of His kingdom; if you take the time to ask God for His direction He will take the time to bring order to your day.

Communication

For I will give you a mouth and wisdom, which
All your adversaries shall not be able to gainsay nor
resist (Luke 21:15).

Everywhere you go you will find people who are not short of their opinions. They say what they think and don't think twice as to whether it makes sense or is offensive. As Christians, we often find ourselves surrounded by adversarial individuals who try to draw us into debates just for the sake of argument. There is no need to fear; continue to study and meditate upon the Word of God. The Holy Ghost will give you the perfect opportunity to say what should be said to silence contrary individuals. They will have no other alternative but to be still, be quiet and/or submit.

Endurance

In your patience possess ye your souls (Luke 21:19).

Endurance is a faith anchor. For there will be many times where you will have to hold on to faith in God's Word and disregard opposing urges and discouraging facts that try to engender defeat and hopelessness. James 1:3–4 reads:

> *Knowing this, that the trying of your faith worketh patience. But let patience have her perfect work, that ye may be perfect and entire, wanting nothing.*

Holding on is not an option for those who expect to receive a reward for their faith. Now the only way to endure is to stay focused on the reward and not the mechanics of the trials. Trials are made to try you and will either strengthen you or expose a weakness. God has made provisions for your success. Allow endurance to anchor your thoughts and Jesus will make sure that you cross the finish line.

Worship

> *But the hour cometh, and now is, when the true worshippers shall worship the Father in spirit and in truth: for the Father seeketh such to worship him. God is a Spirit: and they that worship him must worship him in spirit and in truth* (John 4:23–24).

Every one with a breath in his/her body is commanded to praise God, but you need the Holy Ghost deep down on the inside to worship. Roman 8:9 tells us

> *. . . Now if any man have not the Spirit of Christ, he is none of his.*

The Holy Ghost is the seal that you belong to God which equips you to worship God in "Spirit and in Truth and makes you a true Worshipper".

If you want to experience true worship, get the Holy Ghost, with the evidence of "speaking in other tongues" (Acts 2:4); the influence of the Spirit of God that gives you a heavenly language. Praise is Great; Worship is a *Must!*

Spiritual Sustenance

And Jesus said unto them, I am the bread of life: he that cometh to me shall never hunger; and he that believeth on me shall never thirst (John 6:35).

In Jesus you will find complete spiritual sustenance. His Word feeds and fuels the lighthouse He created inside of you for Him to dwell and use as a beacon to call and draw you and others closer to Him. God's Word's supernatural life healing and life giving properties bring life to the dead areas of our soul. These properties heal and regenerate our spirit so we can live again through out eternity.

Faith (Hebrew 12:2) provides us with the capacity to believe in Him which quenches the thirsting to trust and the longing to depend.

Life can give wealth and affluence but material and social gain will never satisfy our soul. God created you, and He created you for Him. He made that aching place that is always yearning for its Creator. Get to Jesus and let Him do what only He can and that is quench and satisfy your hunger and thirst.

Acceptance

All that the Father giveth me shall come to me; and him that cometh to me I will in no wise cast out (John 6:37).

Rejection is painful. All of us have been scarred by childhood through adult life memories of not being accepted by those valued to be important. We can find healing from these memories when we realize that the most important and valuable relationship in the whole wide world is having a relationship with Jesus. This relationship will supersede all past relationships and heal you from the scars and disappointments left behind.

Jesus will keep you and never leave you. He will be right there in your finest hours and hold you when you are at your worst. Jesus will prove how sovereign His love can be in your life. Romans 8:35–39 reminds us:

> *Who shall separate us from the love of Christ? shall tribulation, or distress, or persecution, or famine, or nakedness, or peril, or sword? As it is written, For thy sake we are killed all the day long; we are accounted as sheep for the slaughter. Nay, in all these things we are more than conquerors through him that loved us. For I am persuaded, that neither death, nor life, nor angels, nor principalities, nor powers, nor things present, nor things to come, Nor height, nor depth, nor any other creature, shall be able to separate us from the love of God, which is in Christ Jesus our Lord.*

Jesus is with us for the long haul; a relationship with Him surpasses all the human rejection of past failed relationships and endures to and throughout eternity.

Life Transforming Power

He that believeth on me, as the scripture hath said,
out of his belly shall flow rivers of living water
(John 7:38).

God transforms everything He comes into contact with. He is the master of taking the fragmented, disjointed broken pieces of your life and bring them together to form an organized sense of purpose. Invite God into the innermost part of your being so He can fill you with the Holy Ghost, transform and pour out of you a continual flow of purpose and power through His Word which will change and transform you and the life of others.

Liberty

Then said Jesus to those Jews which believed on him, If ye continue in my word, then are ye my disciples indeed; And ye shall know the truth, and the truth shall make you free (John 8:31–32).

The Kingdom of God defies the limits of the physical realm of the world and its training to use our senses as the process to determine what is real and true. The Word of God usurps authority over our senses and through the Holy Ghost gives us freedom from the bondages of deception. The Bible clearly states in 2 Corinthians 4:18:

While we look not at the things which are seen, but at the things which are not seen: for the things which are seen are temporal; but the things which are not seen are eternal.

Faith challenges us to press beyond our sensory perceptions and take hold of the Word of God as our object of truth. For the truth of God goes beyond the limitations of this world and causes us to experience the power and liberty of God's unlimited power. Don't be bound by making life's decisions that are based upon mere facts and reasonings. Enjoy the benefits of abundant life which comes from the wealth of knowing and having God's spirit and knowing His truth.

Now the Lord is that Spirit: and where the Spirit of the Lord is, there is liberty (2 Corinthians 3:17)

Abundance

> *I am the door: by me if any man enter in, he shall*
> *be saved, and shall go in and out, and find pasture.*
> *The thief cometh not, but for to steal and to kill,*
> *and to destroy: I am come that they might have*
> *life, and that they might have it more abundantly*
> (John 10:9,10).

There is no mistake in the fact that life has rewards, but God wants to give you more than you've earned. Proverbs 14:23 says:

In all labour there is profit:

Unfortunately, these profits serve only as mere rations of immediate gratification when gained outside the will of God, for the more we get, the more we want and the more we want the greater the price we have to pay to get. Self fulfillment is the catalyst in neglected relationships and the primary agenda of the flesh. You're tricked to believe that you must depend on yourself to be rewarded with the things that you want and need, this further motivates for selfish behavior. These rewards are restrictive, temporary and rob you from the eternal inheritance and provision God has for them that depend and rely upon Him.

Walk with God, allow Him to lead you through His door of abundance. The power of His Word will keep you safe from practices that leave you vulnerable to theft, death and destruction.

Extraordinary

> *Verily, verily, I say unto you, He that believeth on*
> *me, the works that I do shall he do also; and greater*
> *works than these shall he do; because I go unto my*
> *Father. And whatsoever ye shall ask in my name,*
> *that will I do, that the Father may be glorified in*
> *the Son. If ye shall ask any thing in my name, I will*
> *do it. If ye love me, keep my commandment* (John
> 14:12-15).

Exceptional people are often characterized by the extraordinary things they perform. It is discouraging to feel that life has assigned you to the mundane and the ordinary. Such feelings are contrary to the assignment God has given you in His Word. Jesus did great things in His life. He left us an example of just how He wants things to be done around here and He wants YOU to do these things and more. His life and death reconciled us back to the Father, and gave us access to the power and authority of His name. Loving obedience to God will grant you the extraordinary opportunities to live the life of the extraordinary.

Comfort

I will not leave you comfortless: I will come to you
(John 14:18).

God is mindful of everything that you go through and never intended for you to go through them alone. He is with you not just as a silent observer, but with the comfort of His instructions brings you through life's most trying and challenging situations. He wants His Spirit, the very mind of God to live inside of you and be the guiding influence for your life. Invite God to come and stay in your life and His presence will provide you with directions and comfort for living in relationship with the Lord Jesus Christ.

> *Blessed be God, even the Father of our Lord Jesus Christ, the Father of mercies, and the God of all comfort; Who comforteth us in all our tribulation, that we may be able to comfort them which are in any trouble, by the comfort wherewith we ourselves are comforted of God* (2 Corinthians 1:3–4).

Memory

But the Comforter, which is the Holy Ghost,
whom the Father will send in my name, he shall
teach you all things, and bring all things to your
remembrance, whatsoever I have said unto you
(John 14:26).

Life's distractions act as a memory blocker to divert your attention from the promises of God. The Holy Ghost acts a constant reminder that God will "watch over His Word to perform it" (Jeremiah 1:12).

You need the Holy Ghost, the Spirit of God dwelling in you, to teach you and remind you of what God has spoken and the specifics that will come to pass in your life.

God wants you to remember every promise and instruction He has given you. Pray and thank God every day for His promises and take time throughout the day to rehearse the specific promises He has made to you. Seal those promises with the proclamation Elisabeth spoke to Mary in Luke 1:45:

And blessed is she that believed: for there shall be a
performance of those things which were told her
from the Lord.

Harvest

I am the vine, ye are the branches: He that abideth in me, and I in him, the same bringeth forth much fruit: for without me ye can do nothing (John 15:5).

If ye abide in me, and my words abide in you, ye shall ask what ye will, and it shall be done unto you (John 15:7).

Ye have not chosen me, but I have chosen you, and ordained you, that ye should go and bring forth fruit, and that your fruit should remain: that whatsoever ye shall ask of the Father in my name, he may give it you (John 15:16).

The Word of God has been planted in our hearts to yield a supernatural harvest. Continuously sowing God's Word aligns our life to the will of God and provides a healthy connection for our branches to receive the proper nutrients for spiritual growth and development. Growth does not mean maturity. God regulates our process of maturity and we must stay connected to God's process so that we can develop and yield an abundant life of much fruit. If we sever ourselves from the vine we will yield unripe fruit and avert future harvests. Let's stay connected! Seek God's will for your life and obey it for this will transform your will to His and cause you to receive a perpetual harvest in this season and seasons to come.

Holy Ghost

> *Then Peter said unto them, Repent, and be baptized*
> *every one of you in the name of Jesus Christ for the*
> *remission of sins, and ye shall receive the gift of the*
> *Holy Ghost* (Acts 2:38).

Salvation is a gift, but you must participate to receive it. You must acknowledge that you are a sinner and sincerely believe that Jesus died for your sins and is able and willing to forgive you for every sin that you have ever committed in your life. Forgiveness of sins has a purpose which is to create a suitable place for God's Spirit to dwell.

Baptism in the name of Jesus Christ is the physical act that represents the death, burial, and resurrection of Jesus Christ. Romans 6:4 explains:

> *Therefore we are buried with him by baptism into*
> *death: that like as Christ was raised up from the*
> *dead by the glory of the Father, even so we also*
> *should walk in newness of life.*

Once He's forgiven you of your sin, invite Him in to rest, rule and abide and He will give you the Holy Ghost. This Spirit of Life will come in and make you free from the laws of sin and death which formally governed your life (Romans 8:2) and give you a heavenly language (Acts 2:4) that transfers personal prayers, requests and answers to and from the throne of God.

You need the Holy Ghost; it is the distinguishing factor that says you belong to God. Romans 10:9 teaches:

But ye are not in the flesh, but in the Spirit, if so be
that the Spirit of God dwell in you. Now if any man
have not the Spirit of Christ, he is none of his.

Get the Holy Ghost, having God's spirit has eternal consequences that will daily load you with benefits and lead to eternal life.

Benefits of Righteousnesses

Therefore being justified by faith, we have peace with God through our Lord Jesus Christ: By whom also we have access by faith into this grace wherein we stand, and rejoice in hope of the glory of God. And not only so, but we glory in tribulations also: knowing that tribulation worketh patience; And patience, experience; and experience, hope: And hope maketh not ashamed; because the love of God is shed abroad in our hearts by the Holy Ghost which is given unto us (Romans 5:1–5).

Christ has made us right with God and given us the faith to believe that it was done by Him and Him alone. Faith in the atoning work of Christ gives us access to all the benefits of being in right relationship with Him. We have His grace and unmerited favor which enables us to experience unearned blessings. We are thus able to endure life's challenges and while remaining unshaken we can become totally convinced of His love and that Christ is who He says He is and does what He says He can do.

Being in right standing with Christ affords us the privilege to celebrate the process of the battle as well as the sweetness of the triumphant victory.

Hearing, Preaching Faith

> For whosoever shall call upon the name of the Lord shall be saved. How then shall they call on him in whom they have not believed? and how shall they believe in him of whom they have not heard and how shall they hear without a preacher? And how shall they preach, except they be sent? As it is written, How beautiful are the feet of them that preach the gospel of peace, and bring glad tidings of good things! But they have not all obeyed the gospel. For Esaias saith, Lord, who hath believed our report? So then faith cometh by hearing, and hearing by the word of God (Romans 10:13–17).

Hearing the Word of God develops confidence and faith in God. It is paramount that you hear the preached Word for salvation. 1 Corinthians 1:21 tells us:

> For after that in the wisdom of God the world by wisdom knew not God, it pleased God by the foolishness of preaching to save them that believe.

As a result of preaching, God has made salvation available to man. Man's knowledge of nature and the world around him did not draw him to God. So God designed it so that the preached Word of God would convince the soul of man that He needed Christ.

The person that may have preached salvation to you may not have been a preacher, or you may not have experienced God's best from one, none of this nullifies the office of a preacher. Jesus preached salvation and He has placed His Spirit in His preachers to preach salvation unto mankind. You needed the preached Word of God to hear faith in your spirit to get saved and you need that same preached faith to stay saved.

If you are not bed ridden, do not buy into the lie that you can stay home and still have God. Get to a church that has a Holy Ghost filled preacher that will divinely impart and direct a specifically designed Word from God into your life.

God needs preachers to preach faith in God. Ask Him to send faith filled preachers and to show you those around you who are called to preach. Don't run, hide or be surprised if He reveals that it is you!

Transformation

> *I beseech you therefore, brethren, by the mercies of God, that ye present your bodies a living sacrifice, holy, acceptable unto God, which is your reasonable service. And be not conformed to this world: but be ye transformed by the renewing of your mind, that ye may prove what is that good, and acceptable, and perfect, will of God* (Romans 12:1–2).

Sacrificing your desires, ideas and perceptions daily for God's purpose is the exchange required for a transformed regenerated life in Christ. The Word of God transforms your thinking and guides you in the principles of the Kingdom of God. The Holy Ghost gives you the ability to obey and do His will. In order to live a victorious, complete and pleasing life to God, make a conscious effort to fill your day yielding to God and through His Word the Holy Ghost will manifest a change in your life.

Godly Principles

Having then gifts differing according to the grace that is given to us, whether prophecy, let us prophesy according to the proportion of faith; Or ministry, let us wait on our ministering: or he that teacheth, on teaching; Or he that exhorteth, on exhortation: he that giveth, let him do it with simplicity; he that ruleth, with diligence; he that sheweth mercy, with cheerfulness. Let love be without dissimulation. Abhor that which is evil; cleave to that which is good. Be kindly affectioned one to another with brotherly love; in honour preferring one another; Not slothful in business; fervent in spirit; serving the Lord; Rejoicing in hope; patient in tribulation; continuing instant in prayer; Distributing to the necessity of saints; given to hospitality. Bless them which persecute you: bless, and curse not. Rejoice with them that do rejoice, and weep with them that weep. Be of the same mind one toward another. Mind not high things, but condescend to men of low estate. Be not wise in your own conceits. Recompense to no man evil for evil. Provide things honest in the sight of all men. If it be possible, as much as lieth in you, live peaceably with all men. Dearly beloved, avenge not yourselves, but rather give place unto wrath: for it is written, Vengeance is mine; I will repay, saith the Lord. Therefore if thine enemy hunger, feed him; if he thirst, give him drink: for in so doing thou shalt heap coals of fire on his head. Be not overcome of evil, but overcome evil with good (Romans 12:6–21).

God is very concerned about the way we represent ourselves as Christians. He has clear and sound instructions to govern every facet of spiritual lives. We are the light of the world. God wants us to demonstrate His kingdom on earth and be a shining example to draw men to God and His way of doing things. Use these Godly principles as a governing instrument for your every decision and action and you will realize heaven on earth and be the shining example that God has called you to be.

Spiritual Understanding

But as it is written, Eye hath not seen, nor ear heard, neither have entered into the heart of man, the things which God hath prepared for them that love him.

But God hath revealed them unto us by his Spirit: for the Spirit searcheth all things, yea, the deep things of God. For what man knoweth the things of a man, save the spirit of man which is in him? even so the things of God knoweth no man, but the Spirit of God. Now we have received, not the spirit of the world, but the spirit which is of God; that we might know the things that are freely given to us of God.

Which things also we speak, not in the words which man's wisdom teacheth, but which the Holy Ghost teacheth; comparing spiritual things with spiritual.But the natural man receiveth not the things of the Spirit of God: for they are foolishness unto him: neither can he know them, because they are spiritually discerned.

But he that is spiritual judgeth all things, yet he himself is judged of no man. For who hath known the mind of the Lord, that he may instruct him?

But we have the mind of Christ (1 Corinthians 2: 9–16).

There are things that you will only get to know and understand as you develop in the things of God. As in any relationship, the more time you spend with God, the more you understand His desires and plans for your life. Some things He reveals to us at the onset of the relationship, others He specifically reveals as our relationship matures. If you find yourself with questions that seem to keep going unanswered, check and see if you have become stagnate in your walk with Christ. The answer might lie ahead, waiting for you to reach a certain spiritual level of maturity, so you can not only know but also know what to do.

Managing Temptation

There hath no temptation taken you but such as is common to man: but God is faithful, who will not suffer you to be tempted above that ye are able; but will with the temptation also make a way to escape, that ye may be able to bear it (1 Corinthians 10:13).

Ecclesiastes 1:9 tells us that

. . . there is no new thing under the sun.

This scripture destroys the deceptive feeling that you are the only one going through a specific trial or temptation. Let's face some Biblical truths; what you're going through is nothing new, you're not alone and you will get through it! Why? Because the sovereignty of God has ordered your steps, (Psalm 37:23) and God's grace provides you with the ability to endure and escape the trappings and sinful desires of the flesh.

View temptation as motivation to finding and staying in the straight path of God's Word for through His Word you will receive the wisdom and strength to manage temptation.

Unity in the Body of Christ

Now there are diversities of gifts, but the same Spirit. And there are differences of administrations, but the same Lord. And there are diversities of operations, but it is the same God which worketh all in all. But the manifestation of the Spirit is given to every man to profit withal. For to one is given by the Spirit the word of wisdom; to another the word of knowledge by the same Spirit; To another faith by the same Spirit; to another the gifts of healing by the same Spirit; To another the working of miracles; to another prophecy; to another discerning of spirits; to another divers kinds of tongues; to another the interpretation of tongues: But all these worketh that one and the selfsame Spirit, dividing to every man severally as he will.For as the body is one, and hath many members, and all the members of that one body, being many, are one body: so also is Christ. For by one Spirit are we all baptized into one body, whether we be Jews or Gentiles, whether we be bond or free; and have been all made to drink into one Spirit. For the body is not one member, but many. If the foot shall say, Because I am not the hand, I am not of the body; is it therefore not of the body? And if the ear shall say, Because I am not the eye, I am not of the body; is it therefore not of the body? If the whole body were an eye, where were the hearing? If the whole were hearing, where were the smelling? But now hath God set the members every one of them in the body, as it hath pleased him.

And if they were all one member, where were the body? But now are they many members, yet but one body. And the eye cannot say unto the hand, I have no need of thee: nor again the head to the feet, I have no need of you. Nay, much more those members of the body, which seem to be more feeble, are necessary: And those members of the body, which we think to be less honourable, upon these we bestow more abundant honour; and our uncomely parts have more abundant comeliness. For our comely parts have no need: but God hath tempered the body together, having given more abundant honour to that part which lacked: That there should be no schism in the body; but that the members should have the same care one for another. And whether one member suffer, all the members suffer with it; or one member be honoured, all the members rejoice with it. Now ye are the body of Christ, and members in particular. And God hath set some in the church, first apostles, secondarily prophets, thirdly teachers, after that miracles, then gifts of healings, helps, governments, diversities of tongues. Are all apostles? are all prophets? are all teachers? are all workers of miracles? Have all the gifts of healing? Do all speak with tongues? do all interpret? But covet earnestly the best gifts: and yet shew I unto you a more excellent way. (1 Corinthians 12:4–31).

God has designed His Church to operate after the order of the human organism called the body. Ephesians 4:16 further reiterates this principle by stating:

*From whom the whole body fitly joined together
and compacted by that which every joint supplieth,
according to the effectual working in the measure
of every part, maketh increase of the body unto the
edifying of itself in love.*

God created and designed every aspect of the human anatomy to function in divine order to process oxygen and the nutrition from food for healthy development and reproduction of every cell in the body. As in the natural, so in the spirit, the wisdom of God fashioned the church and gave us gifts and abilities, the systems and organs of the spiritual body, which receives and demonstrates the Word of God for the development and reproduction of faith in every healthy believer.

He gave us His Spirit, the breath of life which gives us power to live and operate

> *. . . according to the purpose of him who worketh
> all things after the counsel of his own will:*
> (Ephesians 1:11).

Christ's blood cleanses the body, rids of us our past sins and gives us His righteousness to maintain "a pure heart" and uphold and build the Kingdom of God.

God shaped His Church and every thing He made for it fits in the body for the purpose of growth of the body as a whole. We need every person, every gift, and every administration in the body of Christ to grow. It does not matter whether you are visible or not. We must work together to ensure growth; for if it's not growing, it is dying and neglecting or ignoring some of the smallest symptoms over an extended period of time can result in a major illness than can result in death. The Church also has to pray for Christian ministries and leaderships local and throughout the world, for when one falls and a ministry fails the publicity from it causes the whole body of Christ to suffer.

We must also learn and appreciate this fact in the body of Christ; that if the death, burial and resurrection of our Lord Jesus Christ is the center of a particular church, we must pray for its spiritual health and love and appreciate it. Our focus has to be on whether or not they preach "Jesus as the only Lord and Savior", not their ministry gift strength. Some Pastor's ministry strength is to preach prosperity, some healing and others faith. Some Pastors ministry strength may be to teach administration or finance, while others strengths are to train preachers, teachers and prophets. "We are many members, but one body," we need all these things for kingdom building. If God put it in His Word and it is the "rightly divided Word of Truth, (2 Timothy 2:15) the whole body of Christ needs it!

We will not come into *"the unity of the faith"* (Ephesians 4:13) until we learn to appreciate and respect the different ministries of the body of Christ. So they don't act like us, or dress like us or look like us, so what! A spleen do not look like the heart, the eyes does not look like the toe. The skin is the outward covering for the body; the bladder is an internal organ, situated in the pelvis and is not visible to the naked eye. God gave us skin, it keeps us warm and covers various external parts of the body and helps protect the body from external contaminants. The bladder helps to rid us of the contaminants in the body through the elimination of fluids. Both are very important and if something goes wrong with either one the body is in trouble.

If you have a problem with make-up, women preachers and drums in church and you can't see past these things and see Jesus, you need to get over it. If you can't enjoy a hymn or the preacher because he doesn't "hack" you need to get over it.

This many member body has a ton of different ethnicities and cultures and we need to understand that once we became born again, our race became Christian, our speech became

Christian, we no longer were democratic or republican, but Christian. Our demographics and economics are to portray those of a Christian. Jesus and His Word is our primary focus. Everything else loses its priority and comes under subjection to what unifies the body of Christ, and that is aligning your life with everything that the Word of God calls for us to do and that is to be "Christ like" or a Christian.

Love

Though I speak with the tongues of men and of angels, and have not charity, I am become as sounding brass, or a tinkling cymbal. And though I have the gift of prophecy, and understand all mysteries, and all knowledge; and though I have all faith, so that I could remove mountains, and have not charity, I am nothing. And though I bestow all my goods to feed the poor, and though I give my body to be burned, and have not charity, it profiteth me nothing. Charity suffereth long, and is kind; charity envieth not; charity vaunteth not itself, is not puffed up, Doth not behave itself unseemly, seeketh not her own, is not easily provoked, thinketh no evil; Rejoiceth not in iniquity, but rejoiceth in the truth; Beareth all things, believeth all things, hopeth all things, endureth all things. Charity never faileth: but whether there be prophecies, they shall fail; whether there be tongues, they shall cease; whether there be knowledge, it shall vanish away. For we know in part, and we prophesy in part. But when that which is perfect is come, then that which is in part shall be done away. When I was a child, I spake as a child, I understood as a child, I thought as a child: but when I became a man, I put away childish things. For now we see through a glass, darkly; but then face to face: now I know in part; but then shall I know even as also I am known. And now abideth faith, hope, charity, these three; but the greatest of these is charity (1 Corinthians 13:1–13).

Love has been the subject of many songs, movies and literary pieces which the characters have used as the motive for all types of strange and bizarre behavior. This scripture gives us the true divine nature as to what love is and what it will and will not do. Follow it carefully. I John 4:8 tells us that *"God is Love"*, so trust God and His Word as the final authority as to what love really is.

Perpetual Winner

> *Now thanks be unto God, which always causeth us to triumph in Christ, and maketh manifest the savour of his knowledge by us in every place* (2 Corinthians 2:14).

Being led by God affords us the privilege of coming out of some of the most sticky situations smelling like a rose. Some of these situations may be self inflicted, others may have been traps and most of them are because of weaknesses. "But thanks be unto God", who knows our heart and allows us to repent and be forgiven and through the knowledge of His Word rectifies our wrong to a right standing in Him.

It may be surmised that you didn't get that promotion or your marriage ended up failing, your children may have left the church and the promise God made eight years ago, may not have yet come to pass. Don't fret, God has the last say and He is true to His Word. Take consolation in this promise found in Haggai 2:9.

Your future will be greater than your past.

Guilt Free Living

Therefore if any man be in Christ, he is a new creature: old things are passed away; behold, all things are become new (2 Corinthians 5:17).

Sometimes it seems as if the housewife's most favorite past time is feeling guilty. We feel condemned about not finishing the laundry, we feel guilty about missing the PTA meeting, and we feel badly about being late for picking up the kids. True enough these events are motivations to become more organized and are object lessons from which to learn, but that's the extent of it. Rehearsing these small guilt trips over and over in your mind will lead to a habit of practicing past regrets and failures.

Cut guilt off at the pass; look at every morning as a brand new day of regeneration. Leave all of yesterday's shortcomings and disappointments in the hand of God along with your sincere prayer for forgiveness and strength, for He is in the forgiving and regenerating business which is what you need to live a guilt free life!

Generosity

Now therefore perform the doing of it; that as there was a readiness to will, so there may be a perform-ance also out of that which ye have. For if there be first a willing mind, it is accepted according to that a man hath, and not according to that he hath not (2 Corinthians 8:11–12).

Have you ever had your desire to give not match your ability to give? Take courage, for desire is the basic building block of the foundation of generosity. We serve a generous God who blesses our desire to give with an increase that enables us to give. The more we desire to give the more He gives.

Don't be disheartened by the size of your gift, give it and watch the planted seed of your gift grow into a perennial harvest and become "the gift that keeps on giving"!

Reciprocity

But this I say, He which soweth sparingly shall reap also sparingly; and he which soweth bountifully shall reap also bountifully. Every man according as he purposeth in his heart, so let him give; not grudgingly, or of necessity: for God loveth a cheerful giver. And God is able to make all grace abound toward you; that ye, always having all sufficiency in all things, may abound to every good work: (As it is written, He hath dispersed abroad; he hath given to the poor: his righteousness remaineth for ever. Now he that ministereth seed to the sower both minister bread for your food, and multiply your seed sown, and increase the fruits of your righteousness;) Being enriched in every thing to all bountifulness, which causeth through us thanksgiving to God. For the administration of this service not only supplieth the want of the saints, but is abundant also by many thanksgivings unto God; Whiles by the experiment of this ministration they glorify God for your professed subjection unto the gospel of Christ, and for your liberal distribution unto them, and unto all men; And by their prayer for you, which long after you for the exceeding grace of God in you. Thanks be unto God for his unspeakable gift (2 Corinthians 9:6–15).

Man has devised all kinds of get rich quick prosperity plans which seem to only work for those collecting the money. God wants us to be prosperous. He indicates in 3 John 1:2:

Beloved, I wish above all things that thou mayest prosper and be in health, even as thy soul prospereth.

It is hard to be more direct than that. God's prosperity plan differs from man for where man says make, take and keep, God says:

Give, and it shall be given unto you; good measure, pressed down, and shaken together, and running over, shall men give into your bosom. For with the same measure that ye mete withal it shall be measured to you again (Luke 6:38).

If you want a high yielding return, make a high yielding investment into the Kingdom of God. I like the way our Pastor, Marvin Winans, has taught us, "Sow a natural seed into spiritual soil and you will reap a supernatural harvest!"

Pulling Down Strongholds

> *For though we walk in the flesh, we do not war after the flesh: (For the weapons of our warfare are not carnal, but mighty through God to the pulling down of strong holds;) Casting down imaginations, and every high thing that exalteth itself against the knowledge of God, and bringing into captivity every thought to the obedience of Christ; And having in a readiness to revenge all disobedience, when your obedience is fulfilled* (2 Corinthians 10:3–6).

God has given us His supernatural power to fight against the manipulations and mind games of the enemy. The enemy would try to seduce us to come on his turf and condescend to his carnal attacks of words, emotions and heady mind games. We can ill afford to leave our home court advantage; we must learn to stay on our turf and destroy the works of the flesh through the Word of God. The enemy is a liar who tries to exalt his threats above the Word and the plan God has for our lives. Keep the Word of God fresh in your heart daily, rehearse it, meditate on it and believe it and use it as the measuring instrument to evaluate whether a thought can take up residence in your mind. If the thought does not line up with the Word of God, don't take ownership; get rid of it by meditating on the scripture that opposes that thought.

Don't allow yourself to be provoked to respond with your emotions to people and situations being motivated by the enemy. Allow God to give you strength and the power of His Word to confine and render the demonic attacks powerless.

Reward

> Be not deceived; God is not mocked: for whatsoever
> a man soweth, that shall he also reap. For he that
> soweth to his flesh shall of the flesh reap corrup-
> tion; but he that soweth to the Spirit shall of the
> Spirit reap life everlasting. And let us not be weary
> in well doing: for in due season we shall reap, if we
> faint not (Galatians 6:7–9).

God has a very accurate accounting system and He makes sure
all the things you have done for Him get posted to your account and applies the appropriate "according to the power of
God working in you" interest rate (Ephesians 3:20).

So when you feel like people are taking advantage of you
and those things you do go unnoticed, don't be discouraged.
God sees your obedience and at the determined maturity date
your deposit will yield a supernatural return from your investment into the Kingdom account.

Living Trust

But that no man is justified by the law in the sight of God, it is evident: for, The just shall live by faith (Galatians 3:11).

We live in a performance based society, where he who best follows the rules is heralded the winner. The problem is the rules change day by day and are skewed according to the interpretation of the players. Laws and rules are necessary in life and we must obey them. We must also ensure that we are not doing the right thing just for the sake of being able to brag about our own self-righteousness.

There are not enough good things in the world for us to do that would earn righteousness,

> *for all our righteousness is as filthy rags* (Isaiah 64:4).

Jesus died on the cross and shed His blood to pay the price for our sin, so we can be made right and live by faith in His righteousness. Live a life of trusting in Christ's redemptive work of righteousness, it's less time consuming than trying to work it out on your own!

Standing Firm

*Stand fast therefore in the liberty wherewith Christ
hath made us free, and be not entangled again with
the yoke of bondage* (Galatians 5:1).

The familiarity of your past has a way of wooing you back to
an old comfort zone. Don't give in. The comfort of always
knowing what to do and what to expect is a trap that hinders
you from developing your faith in God. God has delivered you
from co-dependent behaviors and habits from your past. Do
not go back just because you find yourself in unfamiliar territory. Stand firm and remind yourself of your freedom that you
now have in Christ and that no matter what, no past comfort
is worth the pain of the past which held you captive.

Alive Faith

> *I am crucified with Christ: nevertheless I live; yet not I, but Christ liveth in me: and the life which I now live in the flesh I live by the faith of the Son of God, who loved me, and gave himself for me* (Galatians 2:20).

God will not compete with your flesh. Jesus gave His life and paid the ultimate price for us so that our righteousness would be based on our faith in Him and not our ability alone. We must do our part and die to self motivated desires which influence us to make and live by our own decisions. God wants us to have His Spirit so we can live a lifestyle of believing, depending and relying upon His Word for every day life. Christ gave His life for us, we must give our life for Him.

Spirit Walk

This I say then, Walk in the Spirit, and ye shall not fulfil the lust of the flesh. For the flesh lusteth against the Spirit, and the Spirit against the flesh: and these are contrary the one to the other: so that ye cannot do the things that ye would. But if ye be led of the Spirit, ye are not under the law.

Now the works of the flesh are manifest, which are these; Adultery, fornication, uncleanness, lasciviousness, Idolatry, witchcraft, hatred, variance, emulations, wrath, strife, seditions, heresies, Envyings, murders, drunkenness, revellings, and such like: of the which I tell you before, as I have also told you in time past, that they which do such things shall not inherit the kingdom of God. But the fruit of the Spirit is love, joy, peace, longsuffering, gentleness, goodness, faith, Meekness, temperance: against such there is no law. And they that are Christ's have crucified the flesh with the affections and lusts. If we live in the Spirit, let us also walk in the Spirit. Let us not be desirous of vain glory, provoking one another, envying one another" (Galatians 5:16–26).

God makes it plain and clear as to what goes into the lust category and what belongs in the spirit category. Walking in the Spirit requires demonstrating the fruit of the Spirit and not practicing the lust of the flesh. The one has no tolerance for the other. There is a canceling affect between the two, flesh works cancel spiritual fruits and spiritual fruits cancel flesh works.

Make a spiritual note of this scripture to see where your thoughts and deeds line up and make a conscious decision to "walk in the Spirit, so you will not fulfill the lust of the flesh".

Compassion

Brethren, if a man be overtaken in a fault, ye which are spiritual, restore such an one in the spirit of meekness; considering thyself, lest thou also be tempted. Bear ye one another's burdens, and so fulfil the law of Christ (Galatians 6:1, 2).

God does not allow us to observe the faults and failures of others just for information's sake. The enemy tries to get us so impressed with a person's faults and sins so we will fail to take advantage of the Godly opportunity to pray and restore. Lack of spiritual compassion limits us to carnal responses of gossip and offense. Being like Christ requires that we do what He does. We should follow His example and be "moved" by our compassion and keep in mind how we would feel if we were in a similar situation. God has given us His compassion to use for others, we must gravitate to situations to show God's compassion and do our part to ensure that each member of the body of Christ is properly maintained, made whole and operating in their rightful place.

Insight

*That the God of our Lord Jesus Christ, the Father
of glory, may give unto you the spirit of wisdom
and revelation in the knowledge of him: The eyes of
your understanding being enlightened; that ye may
know what is the hope of his calling, and what the
riches of the glory of his inheritance in the saints,
And what is the exceeding greatness of his power to
us-ward who believe, according to the working of
his mighty power* (Ephesians 1:17–19).

This should clear up any doubts you may have and give you a
full assurance that God wants you to be fully aware of your
purpose and destiny. God gives the spirit of wisdom and revelation for accuracy and clarity as to what He wants you to
do and what the rewards are for doing it. God's revelation
confirms our faith and causes us to experience the unlimited
power of God when we allow Him to work in and through
our lives.

You don't have to be confused. Pray and ask God for wisdom and revelation and you will find the confidence and insight you need to follow and obey the Word of God.

*That he would grant you, according to the riches
of his glory, to be strengthened with might by his
Spirit in the inner man; That Christ may dwell in
your hearts by faith; that ye, being rooted and
grounded in love, May be able to comprehend with
all saints what is the breadth, and length, and
depth, and height; And to know the love of Christ,
which passeth knowledge, that ye might be filled*

with all the fulness of God. Now unto him that is able to do exceeding abundantly above all that we ask or think, according to the power that worketh in us (Ephesians 3:16–20).

Right Attitude
Right Motives

I therefore, the prisoner of the Lord, beseech you that ye walk worthy of the vocation wherewith ye are called, With all lowliness and meekness, with longsuffering, forbearing one another in love; Endeavouring to keep the unity of the Spirit in the bond of peace. There is one body, and one Spirit, even as ye are called in one hope of your calling; One Lord, one faith, one baptism, One God and Father of all, who is above all, and through all, and in you all.

But unto every one of us is given grace according to the measure of the gift of Christ (Ephesians 4:1–7).

Being a Christian requires that you do things differently, your perception and "modus operandi" must change from carnal to spiritual. Believer's thinking must be motivated to meet the needs of others. Romans 12:10 tells us:

Be kindly affectioned one to another with brotherly love; in honour preferring one another;

As wives and mothers, generally we know how to make the necessary sacrifices for the welfare of our family. We must also learn to extend these sacrificial principles outside our home. Serving others requires that your preferences take a back seat to the feelings, needs and desires of others. You will need a servant's heart to do this. Ask God to give you a servant's heart and He will give you the gentle patience to do what He says in the right way.

Change

That ye put off concerning the former conversation the old man, which is corrupt according to the deceitful lusts; And be renewed in the spirit of your mind; And that ye put on the new man, which after God is created in righteousness and true holiness (Ephesians 4:22–24).

Changing requires regeneration in thoughts and behaviors. Most change is birthed out of pain. People are not willing to change until what they are in becomes uncomfortable to them. Salvation is a continual process of unlearning old behaviors and thought patterns and learning new ones. Read the Word of God daily and keep it fresh in your heart and watch your normal reactions be transformed into supernatural actions.

Surrender

Wives, submit yourselves unto your own husbands,
as unto the Lord. For the husband is the head of the
wife, even as Christ is the head of the church: and
he is the saviour of the body. Therefore as the
church is subject unto Christ, so let the wives be to
their own husbands in every thing. Husbands, love
your wives, even as Christ also loved the church,
and gave himself for it; That he might sanctify and
cleanse it with the washing of water by the word,
That he might present it to himself a glorious
church, not having spot, or wrinkle, or any such
thing; but that it should be holy and without blem-
ish. So ought men to love their wives as their own
bodies. He that loveth his wife loveth himself. For
no man ever yet hated his own flesh; but nourisheth
and cherisheth it, even as the Lord the church: For
we are members of his body, of his flesh, and of his
bones. For this cause shall a man leave his father
and mother, and shall be joined unto his wife, and
they two shall be one flesh. This is a great mystery:
but I speak concerning Christ and the church. Nev-
ertheless let every one of you in particular so love
his wife even as himself; and the wife see that she
reverence her husband (Ephesians 5:22–33).

It is amazing (although I do not find it surprising) that so many
Christian women find this scripture offensive. I understand
that the wife submitting subject has been an object of abuse in
some Christian circles; inasmuch as we fail to keep in mind

that the body of Christ as a whole has been instructed to "submit one to another" (Ephesians 5:21). This passage of scripture has been given in relationship to how the Christian marriage is to typify the relationship of Jesus and His bride the Church, with love and submission as its foundation.

Don't get bent out of shape when you hear the "S" word; it goes across the board. Submission is the catalyst for unity. In order to be one, someone has to surrender his individual rights. After all, most of us did not mind surrendering our individuality to please our spouses before we were married; we wanted to wear his favorite color, dress and hairstyle. Now if love is to continue to grow our surrender must also continue to increase.

Victory

Finally, my brethren, be strong in the Lord, and in the power of his might. Put on the whole armour of God, that ye may be able to stand against the wiles of the devil. For we wrestle not against flesh and blood, but against principalities, against powers, against the rulers of the darkness of this world, against spiritual wickedness in high places. Wherefore take unto you the whole armour of God, that ye may be able to withstand in the evil day, and having done all, to stand. Stand therefore, having your loins girt about with truth, and having on the breastplate of righteousness; And your feet shod with the preparation of the gospel of peace; Above all, taking the shield of faith, wherewith ye shall be able to quench all the fiery darts of the wicked. And take the helmet of salvation, and the sword of the Spirit, which is the word of God: Praying always with all prayer and supplication in the Spirit, and watching thereunto with all perseverance and supplication for all saints; (Ephesians 6:10–18)

Victory denotes that there has been a winner and a loser. The Bible teaches us in 1 Corinthians 15:57:

But thanks be to God, which giveth us the victory through our Lord Jesus Christ.

Make sure that you are on the right battle ground and in the right war. Christians are not ordained to win wars we are not assigned to fight.

*For though we walk in the flesh, we do not war
after the flesh:* (2 Corinthians 10:3)

Christian warfare is a fight to maintain a victory that has already been won spiritually, totally relying upon God's power to be our strength. His Word is our offensive and defensive strategic training manual and His Blood the seal upon all spiritual protective coverings and weaponry.

The war has been won yet the enemy is still trying to fight. Remind him of his defeat and stay prepared. You cannot use what you don't have, so make sure you have the Holy Ghost, and He will show you when to use the proper maneuvers in God's Word so you can keep the victory and maintain your authority on your territory.

Accomplishment

Being confident of this very thing, that he which hath begun a good work in you will perform it until the day of Jesus Christ: (Philippians 1:6)

Be convinced about God's ability to finish what He started in you. We have all in some time or other become frustrated over starting something that we were not able to finish. Such action does not intimidate God who is not bothered by the limitations of our inconsistencies. In fact He uses them to help us realize our own inability and to reveal the benefits of trusting in His unlimited power. You have exhausted a host of disappointing resources, trust God and use His!

Pure Perception

And this I pray, that your love may abound yet more and more in knowledge and in all judgment; That ye may approve things that are excellent; that ye may be sincere and without offence till the day of Christ; Being filled with the fruits of righteousness, which are by Jesus Christ, unto the glory and praise of God (Philippians 1:9–11).

Love affects judgment. More love, purer judgment. We are required as Christians to be able to discern between a good thing and a good thing from God. Our sincere love and commitment to God takes the visual impulses from our eyes and reroutes them from our brain through the Holy Ghost. This then clears our signals and prevents them from being crossed and provides a Godly perspective of all the things that we encounter. Pure perception is the result of pure love and trust and the ability to see yourself and others through the eyes of God. You too can have the eyes of the Father through the spiritual genetics of being born again with Christ.

Christian Conduct

Only let your conversation be as it becometh the gospel of Christ: that whether I come and see you, or else be absent, I may hear of your affairs, that ye stand fast in one spirit, with one mind striving together for the faith of the gospel;   And in nothing terrified by your adversaries: which is to them an evident token of perdition, but to you of salvation, and that of God (Philippians 1:27–28).

As a body of believers, we are to purpose in our hearts to work together in unity. Psalm 133:1 encourages,

Behold, how good and how pleasant it is for brethren to dwell together in unity!

When we come together with one mind and one goal, the power of God will manifest and nothing will be impossible. Working together in love is a mandate for Christian conduct, for unity in Christ commands a blessing (Psalm 133:1–3).

Humility

Fulfil ye my joy, that ye be likeminded, having the same love, being of one accord, of one mind. Let nothing be done through strife or vainglory; but in lowliness of mind let each esteem other better than themselves. Look not every man on his own things, but every man also on the things of others. Let this mind be in you, which was also in Christ Jesus: Who, being in the form of God, thought it not robbery to be equal with God: But made himself of no reputation, and took upon him the form of a servant, and was made in the likeness of men: And being found in fashion as a man, he humbled himself, and became obedient unto death, even the death of the cross. Wherefore God also hath highly exalted him, and given him a name which is above every name: That at the name of Jesus every knee should bow, of things in heaven, and things in earth, and things under the earth; And that every tongue should confess that Jesus Christ is Lord, to the glory of God the Father (Philippians 2:2–11).

Christ gives us a perfect example of humility and its reward. We are to be determined to make people our priority. Ministry means people, people for whose sins Jesus died. Jesus "humbled himself to the cross and became obedient unto death, even the death of the cross". We should also humble ourselves, crucify our desires to be justified because of the sin of others and make servanthood our job description, for if we all look out for one another, no one will be lacking. Now these goals may seem unobtainable, and they are if you plan on accomplishing them with your own cognitive ability. But you don't have to go this alone. Ask God for His help and He will give you His Spirit to manifest kindness, self-sacrifice and rewards that will far exceed anything you could receive on your own.

Superior Knowledge

Yea doubtless, and I count all things but loss for the excellency of the knowledge of Christ Jesus my Lord: for whom I have suffered the loss of all things, and do count them but dung, that I may win Christ, And be found in him, not having mine own righteousness, which is of the law, but that which is through the faith of Christ, the righteousness which is of God by faith: That I may know him, and the power of his resurrection, and the fellowship of his sufferings, being made conformable unto his death; If by any means I might attain unto the resurrection of the dead.

Not as though I had already attained, either were already perfect: but I follow after, if that I may apprehend that for which also I am apprehended of Christ Jesus. Brethren, I count not myself to have apprehended: but this one thing I do, forgetting those things which are behind, and reaching forth unto those things which are before, I press toward the mark for the prize of the high calling of God in Christ Jesus. Let us therefore, as many as be perfect, be thus minded: and if in any thing ye be otherwise minded, God shall reveal even this unto you" (Philippians 3:8–15).

What price are you willing to pay to really know Jesus? It does not matter whether you are a new convert or have been in the church all your life; it is going to cost you something. You may have to give up confidence in your intelligence, you may have to give up your confidence in the intelligence of those you love and trust, you may have to give up time, energy, career pursuits, friends and loved ones, but know this, it cannot compare to the experience of knowing Christ as your personal Lord and Savior.

An experiential knowledge of Jesus supersedes this world's systems of information and facts. The knowledge that God makes available to the Spirit led believer exposes this world's natural laws as restrictive and futile information. Man's knowledge may compensate you with provisional fame and fortune; but the knowledge of God will increase your today, tomorrow and into your eternity. So what you know may be good, but the knowledge that God has for you is "best."

Perfect Peace

Rejoice in the Lord alway: and again I say, Rejoice.
Let your moderation be known unto all men.
The Lord is at hand. Be careful for nothing; but in
every thing by prayer and supplication with thanks-
giving let your requests be made known unto God.
And the peace of God, which passeth all under-
standing, shall keep your hearts and minds through
Christ Jesus.
Finally, brethren, whatsoever things are true,
whatsoever things are honest, whatsoever things are
just, whatsoever things are pure, whatsoever things
are lovely, whatsoever things are of good report; if
there be any virtue, and if there be any praise, think
on these things. Those things, which ye have both
learned, and received, and heard, and seen in me,
do: and the God of peace shall be with you
(Philippians 4:4–9).

When God tells you not to worry, He also gives you the where-withal to walk in the comfort of His request. He will not ask you to do something that He is not willing to equip you to do. God furnishes the believer with the blueprint to tear down worry and to design/build a quiet and restful prosperity. You are responsible to make your mind available as a suitable con-struction site, purged from impure thoughts and desires. Your building materials will consist of thoughts that are "true, hon-est, just, pure, lovely and of good reports." Sealing your prayer and petition with expectation and thanksgiving insulates your building from the elements of doubt and unbelief. Do not deviate from God's building plan and He will impart perfect peace for daily living.

> *Peace I leave with you, my peace I give unto you: not as the world giveth, give I unto you. Let not your heart be troubled, neither let it be afraid* (John 14:27).

Supernatural Ability

> *I can do all things through Christ which strengtheneth me* (Philippians 4:13).

When God gives you an assignment, He gives you everything you need to do it! No matter how difficult the task, you do not have to rely on what you know, He has given you rights to use His power to perform it. So don't waste any time trying to figure out what you are going to do next. Give God permission to have His way and watch Him work a mighty work through you. Remember the Word of God in Zechariah 4:6

> *. . . Not by might, nor by power, but by my spirit, saith the LORD of hosts.*

> *For it is God which worketh in you both to will and to do of his good pleasure* (Philippians 2:13).

Contentment

But my God shall supply all your need according to his riches in glory by Christ Jesus (Philippians 4:19).

We live in an "immediate gratification" driven society. We want it now, we want it fast and we want it in a hurry. The problem with this philosophy is that the thrill of getting it fades as soon as we get it, because we are expecting to be satisfied by things that can only stimulate. "But my God" in His omniscience knows exactly what you need, exactly when you need it and has an unlimited supply of it. Don't live your life with a drive thru mentality. Allow Jesus to give you a sophisticated palette and you will never go back to carnal fast food again.

Heavenly Aspirations

> *If ye then be risen with Christ, seek those things which are above, where Christ sitteth on the right hand of God. Set your affection on things above, not on things on the earth* (Colossians 3:1–2).

Christians follow Christ and as followers of Christ we believe and do as Christ has done. We don't mix philosophies and opinions. We don't do a little Jesus and a little Buddha. God does not do quotas. You cannot live like hell on Friday and Saturday and expect to go to church on Sunday to balance everything out. You can't just read what you want to read, look at whatever you want at the movies or on TV, and listen to just any kind of music. You have to do the things that exemplify and identify with whom you say you belong. God has sanctified you and made you holy, you have been particularly set aside for the purpose of God himself. He wants to live through you as a light and a witness for others so that they too can be saved and not lost. God has given us His Spirit to guide and help us to have spiritual desires and make Godly decisions.

God does not want to condemn us. He wants to help us get it right. He has given us His Word and His Spirit for direction and guidance. If you have not been doing it right, get it right now and be motivated by this passage of scripture:

> *There is therefore now no condemnation to them which are in Christ Jesus, who walk not after the flesh, but after the Spirit. For the law of the Spirit of life in Christ Jesus hath made me free from the law of sin and death. For what the law could not do, in that it was weak through the flesh, God sending his*

own Son in the likeness of sinful flesh, and for sin, condemned sin in the flesh: That the righteousness of the law might be fulfilled in us, who walk not after the flesh, but after the Spirit. For they that are after the flesh do mind the things of the flesh; but they that are after the Spirit the things of the Spirit. For to be carnally minded is death; but to be spiritually minded is life and peace. Because the carnal mind is enmity against God: for it is not subject to the law of God, neither indeed can be. So then they that are in the flesh cannot please God. But ye are not in the flesh, but in the Spirit, if so be that the Spirit of God dwell in you. Now if any man have not the Spirit of Christ, he is none of his (Romans 8:1–9).

Purpose Driven

And whatsoever ye do, do it heartily, as to the Lord, and not unto men; Knowing that of the Lord ye shall receive the reward of the inheritance: for ye serve the Lord Christ (Colossians 3:23–24).

Do not allow your emotions to govern what you will or will not do. Your emotions are not your bylaws but are for being sensitive and compassionate to others. When you allow them to rule how you feel they become unstable and will fluctuate predicated upon the situation. That is why your feelings cannot be determining factors for doing what you are supposed to do. Your emotions crave stimulations, if they are not stimulated right, they will retaliate.

Pleasing God has to be the focus of all your endeavors for there will be times when God will direct you to show kindness and love to someone who is only capable of hating and hurting. This assignment is definitely a flesh killer, but don't be alarmed for God will reward you and resurrect your spirit so that your life will be more and more in Him and less and less of you. God is not limited to spiritual rewards; He will bless you physically, financially and spiritually now and later. So keep in mind in everything you do to disregard your emotional assessment of the situation and do it in a spirit of excellence, for you are not doing it for man, you are doing it for God so He can get the glory of what He has done for you, and through you.

Wise Communication

Walk in wisdom toward them that are without, re-deeming the time. Let your speech be alway with grace, seasoned with salt, that ye may know how ye ought to answer every man (Colossians 4:5–6).

God knows where you are at all times. He knows with whom you are going to come in contact even before you do. That is why it is so important to stay in fellowship with Christ and to commune with Him throughout the day. He has predestined encounters and there are things He wants said. Fellowship produces an uninhibited flow of the wisdom of God which allows you to know what to say and when to say it. Communing with God does not require long drawn out and over rehearsed prayers. As in any intimate relationship, He wants your undivided attention, so He can share with you the intimacies of His heart and the specific details that you need to fulfill the assignments of your day. Spending time with God will prove to be a benefit to you in the things He wants said to those with whom you come in contact.

Holy Living

Rejoice evermore.

Pray without ceasing.

In every thing give thanks: for this is the will of God in Christ Jesus concerning you. Quench not the Spirit.

Despise not prophesyings. Prove all things; hold fast that which is good. Abstain from all appearance of evil. And the very God of peace sanctify you wholly; and I pray God your whole spirit and soul and body be preserved blameless unto the coming of our Lord Jesus Christ. Faithful is he that calleth you, who also will do it" (I Thessalonians 5:16–24).

Here are seven basic instructions for Holy living, five do's and two don'ts, which are indicative of living for God. Oftentimes we find ourselves trying to defend the position of all the things we supposedly "can't do" as believers to non-believers. It's not so much that we can't, it's that we choose not to. Living for God causes you to lead a full life. God needs us and people need us; we do not have time to be consumed with justifying to non-believers what we can't do.

Our priority is to make sure that we are found doing what God has told us to do when He returns. Living Holy is a daily journey and doing what God wants makes life a trip worth taking.

Deliverance from Enemies

> *Finally, brethren, pray for us, that the word of the Lord may have free course, and be glorified, even as it is with you: And that we may be delivered from unreasonable and wicked men: for all men have not faith. But the Lord is faithful, who shall stablish you, and keep you from evil* (2 Thessalonians 3:1–6).

It's amazing how many enemies you can have just because of your faith in Jesus Christ. There are hundreds of religions practiced in America, but none more targeted by the media, politics and other religions than Christianity. It's no mystery that the enemy hates Christians and tries to influence every medium he can to launch his attacks, but it's nothing that prayer can't handle. God is in the enemy deliverance business. On more than one occasion He delivered the children of Israel and delivering you won't be a problem.

So if you find that you have a enemy that is threatening and seems to have all the authority needed to destroy you, don't fret, for they may soon find themselves being knocked off their high horse to hear a voice from heaven saying "why persecutest thou me?" (Acts 9:4)

National Peace

I exhort therefore, that, first of all, supplications, prayers, intercessions, and giving of thanks, be made for all men; For kings, and for all that are in authority; that we may lead a quiet and peaceable life in all godliness and honesty. For this is good and acceptable in the sight of our God our Saviour (1 Timothy 2:1–3).

Prayer impacts nations and governments. Proverbs 21:1 tells us:

The king's heart is in the hand of the LORD, as the rivers of water: he turneth it whithersoever he will.

When we pray for our families, churches and church leaders we need to include those in governmental authority. They need spiritual guidance to make the right decisions for our country and the rest of the countries around the world. We need to:

Pray for the peace of Jerusalem: they shall prosper that love thee (Psalm 122:6).

There is a blessing for praying for Jerusalem, keep them always in your prayers. This world is in trouble, and it is going to get a lot worse once Jesus raptures us and take us home. While we're here let's pray for the nation's safety for the enemy is all around us waiting for opportunities to perform acts of terrorism. Pray! The more we pray, the safer we are.

Spiritual Instructions for Youth

Let no man despise thy youth; but be thou an example of the believers, in word, in conversation, in charity, in spirit, in faith, in purity. Till I come, give attendance to reading, to exhortation, to doctrine.

Neglect not the gift that is in thee, which was given thee by prophecy, with the laying on of the hands of the presbytery. Meditate upon these things; give thyself wholly to them; that thy profiting may appear to all. Take heed unto thyself, and unto the doctrine; continue in them: for in doing this thou shalt both save thyself, and them that hear thee (1 Timothy 4:12–16).

Salvation may come at any age yet the standard will still remain the same. We teach our children how to walk, talk and tie their shoes. We cannot neglect their spiritual training. The Bible admonishes us to:

Train up a child in the way he should go: and when he is old, he will not depart from it. (Proverbs 22:6).

I live in a Jewish community, and I watch parents walk with their children to the synagogue every Saturday, come rain, snow or sleet. The children walk with their umbrellas or snowsuits, the babies are bundled in their strollers and consistently you see them on their way to the synagogue. This helps me to understand why they are so proud of their heritage; it is imbedded and inbred in them to be proud and not ashamed.

We must also train our children to be proud and not

ashamed of whatever God has called them to do. We must teach them how to cherish it and nurture it. Children being born in this day and time are going to do incredible things for the kingdom. Train your children in the Word of God and you will see the benefits and be able to say "It's in there!"

Immense Increase

But godliness with contentment is great Gain
(1 Timothy 6:6).

This is a Bible principle Word problem.

Godliness + contentment = great gain.

Now this may not make sense in the natural, because most people ascribe contentment with being satisfied and not needing to get or do anything else. Contentment in God is the ability to trust in His sovereignty regardless of your situation.

Unlimited spiritual and physical prosperity which comes from Godly contentment requires a "yielded yes" to God's invitation to reside within and control every aspect of your life. Choosing to live holy and to trust God's promises will increase every aspect of you life. God has promised to take care of everything that you need. Psalm 84:11 says it like this:

For the LORD God is a sun and shield: the LORD will give grace and glory: no good thing will he withhold from them that walk uprightly.

Faith Fight

> *Fight the good fight of faith, lay hold on eternal life,*
> *whereunto thou art also called, and hast professed a*
> *good profession before many witnesses* (1 Timothy
> 6:12).

You publicly confessed Jesus as your Lord and Savior and the goal of that confession is to live forever with God. Stay focused; don't be distracted, the attack is directed at your faith. Don't stand there and allow circumstances to take away your confidence, fight back using the Word of God. The Word of God is your salvation maintenance plan and will fight for you if you use it (Ephesians 6:17), build your faith when you hear it, (Romans 10:17) and direct you if you trust it (Psalm 119:105).

The battle is fought, the victory is won. Maintain your position and fight for the right to believe!

Good Foundation

Charge them that are rich in this world, that they be not highminded, nor trust in uncertain riches, but in the living God, who giveth us richly all things to enjoy; That they do good, that they be rich in good works, ready to distribute, willing to communicate; Laying up in store for themselves a good foundation against the time to come, that they may lay hold on eternal life (1 Timothy 6:17–19).

. . . For unto whomsoever much is given, of him shall be much required: and to whom men have committed much, of him they will ask the more (Luke 12:48).

The greater the reward, the greater the responsibility. God does not bless us just for us, as good stewards, He is looking for an increased return. In order for us to yield an increased harvest, we are required to take the seed that has been given to us and sow it into the soil of others. We have a job to build the kingdom of God and when we invest in others, God continues to invest in us on earth with earthly and spiritual blessings.

Spiritual Development

Wherefore I put thee in remembrance that thou stir up the gift of God, which is in thee by the putting on of my hands (2 Timothy 1:6).

In life you will experience good days and what may feel like not so good days. Do not be discouraged and allow yourself to become stagnate in your purpose by events that may not have gone the way you had planned. Use disappointments as fuel, burn them and allow them to move you closer to the plans God has for your life. Don't waste time on regret which makes you apprehensive and causes you to shy away from pursuing your purpose. Stand on the Word of God Who has enabled you with His Spirit and given you the ability to love when it is hard, persevere when it is difficult and maintain self control when things seem to be out of control. Life is a process, be confident for He will bring you to your "expected end" (Jeremiah 29:11) in the process of time.

Fear Remover

For God hath not given us the spirit of fear; but
of power, and of love, and of a sound mind
(2 Timothy 1: 7).

No one likes feeling afraid, but yet we saturate ourselves with images of horror, suspense and fear, all for the sake of entertainment. Unfortunately we fail to realize that fear is a predatory spirit and cannot be confined to recreational use. You may have innocently invited fear through a horror film, but once inside it invades your soul and attaches to feed upon the emotions and insecurities of your psyche.

God does not desire for you to be fearful. Guard against subtle fear invasions by avoiding content containing fear. Study specific scriptures pertaining to God's power and love, for the Word will direct your thought life and help you develop discipline to recognize and defeat the spirit of fear.

Spiritual Confidence

For the which cause I also suffer these things: never-theless I am not ashamed: for I know whom I have believed, and am persuaded that he is able to keep that which I have committed unto him against that day (2 Timothy 1:12).

Confidence in God is the act of being convinced despite your circumstances that God can and will do what He says. So when you find yourself smack dab in the middle of confusion, place your life in His hands and remember:

And we know that all things work together for good to them that love God, to them who are the called according to his purpose (Romans 8:28).

Sustained Purpose

That good thing which was committed unto thee keep by the Holy Ghost which dwelleth in us (2 Timothy1:14).

As a member of the body of believers, you have been commissioned for assignment. This mission may include the use of your natural talent and abilities, but don't be tricked, you need the power of the Holy Ghost to carry out your purpose. God pre-designed you and gave you specific abilities to perform specific tasks. Your ability alone will only reap temporary success. The Holy Ghost will produce future and eternal rewards. Allow the Holy Ghost to sustain you and keep you "on point", for a gift outside of Christ will lift you up only so far and for only so long.

Spiritual Fortitude

Thou therefore endure hardness, as a good soldier
of Jesus Christ. No man that warreth entangleth
himself with the affairs of this life; that he may
please him who hath chosen him to be a soldier.
And if a man also strive for masteries, yet is he not
crowned, except he strive lawfully. The husbandman
that laboureth must be first partaker of the fruit
(2 Timothy 2:3–7).

You have been enlisted into the Army of the Lord and there is no room for drifters. Orders must be followed to a tee to prevent loss of life. Warfare is not an easy job so you must be attentive regardless of what is going on around you.

The war has been won therefore settle the issue on your soul's battle ground and "fight the good fight of faith" and you will be promoted from an observer to a "first hand" experiential faith in Jesus Christ.

Diligent Workman

Study to shew thyself approved unto God, a work-man that needeth not to be ashamed, rightly divid-ing the word of truth (2 Timothy 2:15).

You have to know what God says in order to say what God says. To study God's Word, you first have to know God. You need His Spirit to know His intent. Ask God for understand-ing when you read His Word; write it down and commit it to memory. Dig deeply and study the original language and see what God was saying through His writers and what purpose or situation was being addressed. The more time you spend with God and His Word the more He will reveal to you. Study to know God and not to impress others. Seek Christ through the scriptures and you will receive God's stamp of approval, an accurate wealth of knowledge, wisdom and revelation of who He is.

Sure Foundation

Nevertheless the foundation of God standeth sure, having this seal, The Lord knoweth them that are his. And, Let every one that nameth the name of Christ depart from iniquity (2 Timothy 2:19).

The atoning death of Jesus Christ on the cross restored man back in right relationship with God and began the building of His Church; the people of the Kingdom of God. Jesus, the chief cornerstone, has built His church upon the foundation of the spoken Word, through His prophets and apostles (Ephesians 2:20) and has called and sealed us with His righteousness so we no longer are enslaved to our sin nature and its debt.

We are sealed with the righteousness of Christ. Proclaim Jesus as "Lord and Savior" and leave your sin nature nailed to the cross for a sure foundation that will withstand the wind and tides of false religions and erroneous doctrines.

Now therefore ye are no more strangers and foreigners, but fellow citizens with the saints, and of the household of God; And are built upon the foundation of the apostles and prophets, Jesus Christ himself being the chief corner stone; In whom all the building fitly framed together groweth unto an holy temple in the Lord: In whom ye also are builded together for an habitation of God through the Spirit (Ephesians 2:19–22).

Evangelism

And the servant of the Lord must not strive; but be gentle unto all men, apt to teach, patient, In meekness instructing those that oppose themselves; if God peradventure will give them repentance to the acknowledging of the truth; And that they may recover themselves out of the snare of the devil, who are taken captive by him at his will (2 Timothy 2:24–26).

Proverbs 11:30 tells us;

The fruit of the righteous is a tree of life; and he that winneth souls is wise.

When you are sharing the Word of God with others, you are trying to impart a spiritual message to an unregenerate heart. You need the wisdom of God to know what you should say. Sinners are accustomed to being beaten up and down. God wants us to demonstrate Him when we are talking and trying to win souls. Learning the Word of God will build your confidence in the scriptures, therefore combine this with the gift to teach and the Godly characteristics of meekness, patience and gentleness. Then you will have the makings of a wise soul winner able to share the Gospel of Jesus Christ and to navigate the lost to the place in God where they can be found.

Good Deeds

All scripture is given by inspiration of God, and is profitable for doctrine, for reproof, for correction, for instruction in righteousness: That the man of God may be perfect, throughly furnished unto all good works (2 Timothy 3:16–17).

The Bible is the divine Word of God that transcends all barriers and fulfills the most basic needs. There is nothing that the Word of God cannot accomplish. The Bible says in Isaiah 55:11:

So shall my word be that goeth forth out of my mouth: it shall not return unto me void, but it shall accomplish that which I please, and it shall prosper in the thing whereto I sent it.

The Word will do just what God wants, through whomever He chooses. It will fill any void in your life and will inspire confidence to do Godly things that you never would have imagined yourself capable of doing. God has given us His Word to completely equip us with everything we need to do His will.

Don't settle for anything less; get all God has for you through the knowledge of His Word so you can experience a life filled with good works.

Christian Testimony

I have fought a good fight, I have finished my course, I have kept the faith: Henceforth there is laid up for me a crown of righteousness, which the Lord, the righteous judge, shall give me at that day: and not to me only, but unto all them also that love his appearing (2 Timothy 4:7–8).

The testimony that all believers should have on judgment day is "God, I did what you told me to do". There will be no space for excuses or explanations, you either did it, or you didn't. Start today to take inventory of your life to make sure that you are in line with what God has asked you to do and you will be in the line with those who will hear the Lord say:

. . . Well done, thou good and faithful servant: thou hast been faithful over a few things, I will make thee ruler over many things: enter thou into the joy of thy Lord. (Matthew 25:21)

Preservation

> *And the Lord shall deliver me from every evil work, and will preserve me unto his heavenly kingdom: to whom be glory for ever and ever. Amen* (2 Timothy 4:18).

---

1 Peter 5:8 tells us to:

> *Be sober, be vigilant; because your adversary the devil, as a roaring lion, walketh about, seeking whom he may devour:*

There are always plans and hidden agenda being plotted out against the child of God. We are not always aware of these plots, but we can be confident that God is. We are not to be consumed with the fiery darts of the wicked, because God has provided us with the faith in His Word to extinguish all of the enemy's attacks (Ephesians 6:16). So if you ever find yourself being bombarded with thoughts of fear because of the threats and schemes of those who despise you, don't fret because God will deliver and preserve you from all hindrances that want to prevent you from fulfilling your purpose and destiny.

God has all power; He can flip the script and make your enemies buy your dinner (Psalm 23:5) and be at peace with you (Proverbs 16:7).

Character Assignment

But speak thou the things which become sound doctrine: That the aged men be sober, grave, temperate, sound in faith, in charity, in patience.

The aged women likewise, that they be in behaviour as becometh holiness, not false accusers, not given to much wine, teachers of good things; That they may teach the young women to be sober, to love their husbands, to love their children, To be discreet, chaste, keepers at home, good, obedient to their own husbands, that the word of God be not blasphemed (Titus 2:1–10).

God assigns responsibilities and behaviors along with tasks which are a reflection of Christ to those we influence. Each day our lives should represent activities that exemplify holiness. We should examine ourselves and ask "Am I living like a Christian? Is this what a Christian looks like? Would I like those important to me to practice these habits? The answers to these questions should all be "yes!" We must be aware that behavior is a spiritual seed that can be passed down and planted into the lives of those we love, and even though we may have only exemplified an occasional temper flare up we must remember that that seed planted in tender soil could harvest into an aggressive violent behavior. Complete the assignments that God has ordained for your life, pattern your behavior after Him, for you never know which mistake the people around you will learn to do instead of learn from.

Spirit of Joy

Thou hast loved righteousness, and hated iniquity; therefore God, even thy God, hath anointed thee with the oil of gladness above thy fellows (Hebrews 1:9).

There is a blessing in loving what God loves and hating what God hates. When you have purposed in your heart to be governed by righteousness; being fair, just and separate from those who practice partiality and bias, God celebrates the Him He sees in you and rewards you with His Spirit of joy. The Spirit of joy makes you cheerful, pleasant and welcoming. People enjoy being around you and you find yourself operating in the gift of hospitality. Embrace the gift that God has given you, for you have been chosen to demonstrate God's open arms to spread joy and welcome to His people.

The Word Benefits

For unto us was the gospel preached, as well as unto them: but the word preached did not profit them, not being mixed with faith in them that heard it (Hebrews 4:2).

The Word of God has been assigned to affect every facet of our life. Every Sunday the preached Word transcends various cultural, economic, racial and gender differences and meets the needs of people on an individual faith basis. The Word of God works. If you want it to work for you make a commitment to Jesus and believe that every word that He has said is true and watch the power of God in you exceed supernaturally beyond what you could ask or think (Ephesians 3:20).

Tranquility

There remaineth therefore a rest to the people of God. For he that is entered into his rest, he also hath ceased from his own works, as God did from his.

Let us labour therefore to enter into that rest, lest any man fall after the same example example of unbelief (Hebrews 4:9–11).

Our days are under a barrage of endless domestic duties which constantly encroach upon wife and mommy time constraints and limited budget allowances. If unchecked our time for meditation in the Word, would be choked out by these "cares of this world" (Matthew 13:22). God has given us insight and provision to fulfill all the needs of the day but this can only be achieved when we rely on God to give us direction. This reliance gives us a rest in our spirit and refreshes us to keep things in proper perspective while rejuvenating us so we can complete tomorrow's tasks.

Don't deprive yourself of the rest that God has provided you; make every effort to spend time with God, for He wants to bring order to your day so you can relax and have confidence that everything that you were supposed to do, God enabled you to get done.

Insight

> *For the word of God is quick, and powerful, and sharper than any two edged sword, piercing even to the dividing asunder of soul and spirit, and of the joints and marrow, and is a discerner of the thoughts and intents of the heart. Neither is there any creature that is not manifest in his sight: but all things are naked and opened unto the eyes of him with whom we have to do* (Hebrews 4:12, 13).

The Word of God is powerful, alive and penetrating and there is nothing that can be done to take away from its efficacy. The enemy cannot stop the Word of God, so he tries to stop you by diverting your attention away from the Word to your perceptual and problem-solving ability. Unfortunately, when we chose to cognitively assess our situations, we factor out the spiritual truth that is revealed through the Word of God.

Never trust in your ability alone, because there is always more than meets the "natural" eye.

Allow God to give you "His sight" through His Word and you will comprehend motives instead of mere facts.

Spiritual Intimacy

> *Seeing then that we have a great high priest, that is passed into the heavens, Jesus the Son of God, let us hold fast our profession. For we have not an high priest which cannot be touched with the feeling of our infirmities; but was in all points tempted like as we are, yet without sin. Let us therefore come boldly unto the throne of grace that we may obtain mercy, and find grace to help in time of need* (Hebrews 4:14–16).

God became flesh, so He is very familiar with its weaknesses and frailties. He is not overwhelmed with your temptations and sins, for no matter who you are or what you've done, all your sin falls under I John 2:16;

> *. . . the lust of the flesh, and the lust of the eyes, and the pride of life.*

Sin is nothing new; Jesus was tempted by it, lived a life without it and died to pay the price for the consequences of it. He experienced all of this so you can freely come to Him and be free from the bondages of sin.

Don't allow sin to keep you out of fellowship with Christ and affect your confession of faith. Do not hesitate; run to Jesus and load up on His daily benefits and don't feel guilty, it's all paid for!

Soul Anchor

> *Wherein God, willing more abundantly to shew unto the heirs of promise the immutability of his counsel, confirmed it by an oath: That by two immutable things, in which it was impossible for God to lie, we might have a strong consolation, who have fled for refuge to lay hold upon the hope set before us: Which hope we have as an anchor of the soul, both sure and stedfast, and which entereth into that within the veil;* (Hebrews 6:17–19).

We have many reasons to be confident in what God says. He is all powerful, all knowing and everywhere at all times and this alone makes Him far superior than all physical and supernatural beings combined. Our experience with God gives us a deeper revelation of who He is and how unlimited He can be in our lives. He seals His love for us with the most comforting promise; "You can trust Me because I can't lie and I won't change!" Everything that He has said He can do, He does and does it effortlessly, and seeks opportunity to do even more for all those who have faith to believe that He will do it for them. God wants us to experience the ultimate relationship with

"The Father who can keep all His promises!"

Fulfilled Promises

*Cast not away therefore your confidence, which
hath great recompence of reward. For ye have need
of patience, that, after ye have done the will of God,
ye might receive the promise. For yet a little while,
and he that shall come will come, and will not tarry.*

*Now the just shall live by faith: but if any man
draw back, my soul shall have no pleasure in him*
(Hebrews 10:35–39).

God has assured us that He will perform His Word, yet we
must realize that most promises require a process and successfully completing the process requires the right attitude. Fear,
complaints and doubts are a sure way to course repetition.
Trust, praise and peace will get you an "A".

The promise far out weighs whatever you have to go
through. Be mindful that your attitude influences the length of
the process.

Be determined to allow faith in God to be your main focus
and before you know it your reward will manifest and far exceed your expectation.

*Now faith is the substance of things hoped for, the
evidence of things not seen* (Hebrews 11:1).

Reward of Faith

But without faith it is impossible to please him: for he that cometh to God must believe that he is, and that he is a rewarder of them that diligently seek him (Hebrews 11:6).

When you know someone who is capable and has a desire to fulfill your request and all you have to do is be persistent, motivation is not difficult. The same is with God. He knows what's in you because He put it in you, and you do not have to prove to Him how much you want it, because He knows how much you want it. God wants you to practice a very important Christian attribute and that is diligence. Diligence develops character and self control which is why He rewards you with some things sooner than others.

Don't allow delay to make you doubt God. The Blesser wants you to be blessed by the blessing so thank Him for allowing you to be committed to the promise and appreciate the fact that He is actively involved in the development of your diligence.

Authentic Faith

> *Wherefore seeing we also are compassed about with so great a cloud of witnesses, let us lay aside every weight, and the sin which doth so easily beset us, and let us run with patience the race that is set before us, Looking unto Jesus the author and finisher of our faith; who for the joy that was set before him endured the cross, despising the shame, and is set down at the right hand of the throne of God* (Hebrews 12:1–2).

At 6 AM prayer at my church you can hear Pop Winans praying "Have mercy O God, for we have never been this way before". Once he says it, you can feel the underlying burden that has secretly attached itself to you during the week and the anxiety of trying to identify it, lift and release a prayer flow into a language that only God and His Spirit understands. Afterwards you feel charged and released for praise, worship and expectation for the 10:45 morning worship service.

God knows the journey that you're on. (Job 23:10) and He wants you to take comfort in the fact that although it may seem unfamiliar, it is not unfamiliar to Him and He has successfully brought a holy heritage of people down the same path. Your faith in God will sustain you throughout this process; this faith is given to you from God.

Your faith has been seeded in your spirit and He is bringing you through circumstances to develop and strengthen your confidence in it. Your faith in God is "the real thing". God started it, He preserves it and He will complete it to bring you to your purpose and destiny in Him.

Peaceable Fruit of Righteousness

And ye have forgotten the exhortation which speaketh unto you as unto children, My son, despise not thou the chastening of the Lord, nor faint when thou art rebuked of him: For whom the Lord loveth he chasteneth, and scourgeth every son whom he receiveth. If ye endure chastening, God dealeth with you as with sons; for what son is he whom the father chasteneth not? But if ye be without chastisement, whereof all are partakers, then are ye bastards, and not sons. Furthermore we have had fathers of our flesh which corrected us, and we gave them reverence: shall we not much rather be in subjection unto the Father of spirits, and live?

For they verily for a few days chastened us after their own pleasure; but he for our profit, that we might be partakers of his holiness. Now no chastening for the present seemeth to be joyous, but grievous: nevertheless afterward it yieldeth the peaceable fruit of righteousness unto them which are exercised thereby. Wherefore lift up the hands which hang down, and the feeble knees;

And make straight paths for your feet, lest that which is lame be turned out of the way; but let it rather be healed. Follow peace with all men, and holiness, without which no man shall see the Lord: (Hebrews 12:5–11).

We live in a day and age where discipline is equated with

abuse and although abuse is very real it cannot be allowed to nullify the need for discipline. Christians should always be aware that the flesh wants to act contrary to the Spirit. To prevent outbursts of the flesh, the spirit has to be in control. Only then will we be able to hear and understand correction which rids us of unproductive flesh works. Trying to understand the discomforts of chastening outside of the spirit, will lead to irritation and frustration. The Spirit understands and finds peace in the process of righteousness, and how the Holy Ghost and the Word of God is needed to keep you in check and in line with God.

The flesh is a mess; it is contrary, rebellious and sensitive to anything or anyone that will not allow it to do what it wants to do. If you find yourself agitated and you just can't put a finger on why, take a look into the scriptures and you may see your flesh being corrected by the Word. Don't be discouraged or become angry when the Word of God comes across the pulpit and cuts through your flesh; God is performing major spiritual surgery to remove your cancerous carnal behavior. Be glad that God is getting everything out that is causing you to be spiritually ill. God is making you whole again, so you can be holy and without blemish which will be the only way you can see the Lord.

> *That he might present it to himself a glorious*
> *church, not having spot, or wrinkle, or any such*
> *thing; but that it should be holy and without*
> *blemish* (Ephesians 5:27).

Joyful Account

Obey them that have the rule over you, and submit yourselves: for they watch for your souls, as they that must give account, that they may do it with joy, and not with grief: for that is unprofitable for you (Hebrews 13:17).

Everyone wants to be the recipient of a good report. We posture ourselves to be seen in the right place doing the right things hoping the right people will see us. But no matter how aggressive the public relations, if you have a hidden agenda and wrong motives God will reveal it to those He has assigned to be responsible for your soul. You cannot slip and slide, nor run and hide; you are important to God and He wants you to get it right. Follow the holy instructions of your pastor, who has been assigned to pray and train you in things pertaining to the Kingdom of God.

Your pastors want the testimony that they did as God instructed. You need the same testimony too, so you can inherit the Kingdom on God on earth and eternal life in heaven.

Tried Patience

> *My brethren, count it all joy when ye fall into divers temptations; Knowing this, that the trying of your faith worketh patience. But let patience have her perfect work, that ye may be perfect and entire, wanting nothing* (James 1:2–4).

The right perspective is paramount to patience. See your struggles and temptations as vehicles to take you to your next level in Christ. See them as resistance training, developing toned spiritual muscles that will allow you to take more, get more and give more. Learning to endure with the right attitude develops character and integrity; spiritual foundational pillars which will sustain exponential levels of success and insure your longevity and weather life storms.

Embedded Word

Wherefore, my beloved brethren, let every man be swift to hear, slow to speak, slow to wrath: For the wrath of man worketh not the righteousness of God. Wherefore lay apart all filthiness and super-fluity of naughtiness, and receive with meekness the engrafted word, which is able to save your souls (James 1:19–21).

The soil of your heart must be amended and enriched in order for the Word of God to take root in your life. If we allow, certain experiences will drain, harden and prevent us from receiving what we need to grow and develop. Be proactive and not reactive; instead of responding out of your emotions, be still, be quiet and listen to what the Spirit has to say. Do not allow your imagination to run away and make its own assessments. Spiritual surrender is the fertile soil that embraces the seed of the Word. The warmth of love from the Son develops the roots and branches, and yields a harvest of spiritual fruits of righteousness.

Allow the Word of God to supersede your emotional desires and you will experience a change in your heart, your mind and your will.

Working Faith

What doth it profit, my brethren, though a man say he hath faith, and have not works? can faith save him? If a brother or sister be naked, and destitute of daily food, And one of you say unto them, Depart in peace, be ye warmed and filled; notwithstanding ye give them not those things which are needful to the body; what doth it profit? Even so faith, if it hath not works, is dead, being alone. Yea, a man may say, Thou hast faith, and I have works: shew me thy faith without thy works, and I will shew thee my faith by my works. Thou believest that there is one God; thou doest well: the devils also believe, and tremble. But wilt thou know, O vain man, that faith without works is dead? Was not Abraham our father justified by works, when he had offered Isaac his son upon the altar? Seest thou how faith wrought with his works, and by works was faith made perfect? (James 2:14–22).

Faith is animated, it is alive, it moves and it brings about change. There must be action to support your confession. The spirit realm attaches itself to your words so that whatever you are saying demands a spiritual response. That spiritual response moves you to move for God. Talk is not cheap, it is very expensive. Make sure that you match your confession with your spiritual compassion and finish the work that God has released out of your spirit so that you may be a blessing to all the people God has called you to reach.

Godly Wisdom

> *But the wisdom that is from above is first pure, then peaceable, gentle, and easy to be intreated, full of mercy and good fruits, without partiality, and without hypocrisy* (James 3:17).

We are taught to believe that information is knowledge and being able to accurately apply knowledge is wisdom. But Spiritual wisdom requires further characterization. Spiritual wisdom has attributes that are diametrically opposed to earthly wisdom. If your wisdom does not line up with these characteristics, it is earthly wisdom which may cause you to be bitter, jealous, with selfish ambitious, out of control and under the influence of the evil around us. Use this Word as a guide for Godly wisdom and allow it to rule your spirit and bring order to your life.

> *If any of you lack wisdom, let him ask of God, that giveth to all men liberally, and upbraideth not; and it shall be given him. But let him ask in faith, nothing wavering. For he that wavereth is like a wave of the sea driven with the wind and tossed. For let not that man think that he shall receive any thing of the Lord* (James 1: 5–8).

Power of Submission

> *Submit yourselves therefore to God. Resist the devil,*
> *and he will flee from you. Draw nigh to God, and*
> *he will draw nigh to you. Cleanse your hands, ye*
> *sinners; and purify your hearts, ye double minded.*
> *Be afflicted, and mourn, and weep: let your laughter*
> *be turned to mourning, and your joy to heaviness.*
> *Humble yourselves in the sight of the Lord, and he*
> *shall lift you up* (James 4:7–10).

Submission is not merely yielding to the knowledge of who God is; you must also be willing to obey Him. Obeying God enables you to refuse the enemy's influences and forces him to leave you alone. Pleasing God creates a desire to be closer to Him. The more you submit, the more He will conform you to His image and likeness so you can come closer. Never be satisfied and become self confident with where you are in Christ. Recognize that a "broken and humble spirit" will always be in need of repair and enablement from the Holy Ghost.

Your reliance and submission will move God to elevate you above your situations and:

> *seat you in heavenly places with Christ Jesus*
> (Ephesians 2:6).

Prescription for Deliverance

Is any among you afflicted? let him pray. Is any merry? let him sing Psalms. Is any sick among you? let him call for the elders of the church; and let them pray over him, anointing him with oil in the name of the Lord: And the prayer of faith shall save the sick, and the Lord shall raise him up; and if he have committed sins, they shall be forgiven him. Confess your faults one to another, and pray one for another, that ye may be healed. The effectual fervent prayer of a righteous man availeth much (James 5:13–16).

The Word of God gives a prescription for deliverance and prevention for the "common cold" ailments of the Spirit.

CONDITION	PRESCRIPTION	CURE
Hard times	Prayer	Provisions
Cheerfulness	Songs of Joy	Rejoicing
Sickness	Call for elders for anointing with oil	Lord raises up
Sinful Acts	Confession	Restoration
Defeatism	Lift up eyes to the hills	Help comes from the Lord

This prescription when taken in its proper dosage will heal, set free and deliver. Keep handy and use as preventive maintenance or at the first sign of "spiritual cough or cold" symptoms.

Growth in Salvation

Wherefore laying aside all malice, and all guile, and hypocrisies, and envies, and all evil speakings, As newborn babes, desire the sincere milk of the word, that ye may grow thereby (Peter 2:1–2).

As in the physical, spiritual growth requires ingestion, digestion, and then emission. You must first ingest the Word of God by studying, hearing and reading it. For proper digestion you must pray over it and ask God for understanding and application. Then follows emission, allowing the Word to drive out and rid you of fleshly contaminations that hinder and limit the healthy application of Bible based principles. Make sure you do everything to get and keep the Word of God active in your life to experience a steady growth in your salvation.

Christian Profession

But ye are a chosen generation, a royal priesthood, an holy nation, a peculiar people; that ye should shew forth the praises of him who hath called you out of darkness into his marvellous light: (1 Peter 2:6–10).

We have been called from living in our lower base nature into living the "high life" in Christ. We are royalty, we're different and we are to act in accordance to our elevated spiritual position. We are no longer obligated to our prior enslaved behavior, now we can assimilate to being like Christ and demonstrate the obvious change of holy living. Living a transformed holy life is an illustration of God's glory and a testimony to all those who have known our past and can recognize the undeniable change from the life we once lived to the Godly life we now live.

Yielded Power

Likewise, ye wives, be in subjection to your own
husbands; that, if any obey not the word, they also
may without the word be won by the conversation
of the wives; While they behold your chaste conver-
sation coupled with fear (1 Peter 3:1–2).

Jeremiah 32:27 reads:

Behold, I am the LORD, the God of all flesh: is
there any thing too hard for me?

For all the women of God who are frightened by the
thought of yielding power to their husbands, take comfort, because God is the God of all flesh. God is the head of man; man
is the head of his house. We as women of God must make sure
that we keep the right attitude and maintain a right relationship with God by recognizing and having a complete understanding of our position.

I Peter 3:4 instructs us on how to sustain our influence.
It reads,

But let it be the hidden man of the heart, in that
which is not corruptible, even the ornament of a
meek and quiet spirit, which is in the sight of God
of great price.

There is nothing subservient to having influence with God
who is over everything and everyone. Your power is in the
prayer that you pray for those who make decisions that affect
you and your family. There is no need for confrontation or dis-

pute. Allow God to give you the peace and quiet you need to walk in the Word of God which promises blessings and destroys curses and you will find comfort in the obedience to yielded power.

Enjoying Every Day Life

For he that will love life, and see good days, let him refrain his tongue from evil, and his lips that they speak no guile: Let him eschew evil, and do good; let him seek peace, and ensue it. For the eyes of the Lord are over the righteous, and his ears are open unto their prayers: but the face of the Lord is against them that do evil (1 Peter 3:10–12).

This is the formula for "the best days for the rest of your life": avoid malicious and immoral conversation, be kind, be good, look for opportunities to follow the path of peace and stay on it. God is looking for every opportunity to reward those who are in right relationship with Him. Do good, for there is a blessing in it.

Ready Response

> *But sanctify the Lord God in your hearts: and be ready always to give an answer to every man that asketh you a reason of the hope that is in you with meekness and fear: Having a good conscience; that, whereas they speak evil of you, as of evildoers, they may be ashamed that falsely accuse your good conversation in Christ* (1 Peter 3:15–16).

There are few greater comforts than knowing and demonstrating what you are proclaiming in the Gospel. God promised us in Matthew 10:19–20:

> *But when they deliver you up, take no thought how or what ye shall speak: for it shall be given you in that same hour what ye shall speak. For it is not ye that speak, but the Spirit of your Father which speaketh in you.*

Wow! How I love Jesus! He promised to give us what to say on His behalf, for we are not justifying our position, we are taking God's position. Who better to give understanding of the Word of God than the author who wrote it? Celebrate your King, for you don't have to make excuses or explain anything, for God will speak for Himself. Your responsibility is to stay tuned to God, live a holy life and say only what He says.

Alarm Proof

> Beloved, think it not strange concerning the fiery
> trial which is to try you, as though some strange
> thing happened unto you: But rejoice, inasmuch as
> ye are partakers of Christ's sufferings; that, when
> his glory shall be revealed, ye may be glad also with
> exceeding joy (1 Peter 4:12–13).

Don't be tricked! You have taken a position to be on the Lord's side, so the enemy is going to attack to make you cower from your stance and prove you wrong. But, as usual he's a liar; his strategy has been exposed and flipped to work on your behalf. As the saying goes "knowing is half the battle". Thank God for giving you the "heads up" concerning your fiery trials. Knowing what's up helps you to look up and see what lies ahead in your destination.

Reaching Your Set Time

Humble yourselves therefore under the mighty hand of God, that he may exalt you in due time: Casting all your care upon him; for he careth for you. Be sober, be vigilant; because your adversary the devil, as a roaring lion, walketh about, seeking whom he may devour: (1 Peter 5:6–8).

You are on target to your destination; don't allow your failures and successes to influence you to take matters into your own hands. Seeking God has gotten you this far, so don't stop now; keep doing what it took to get you where you are today. When you feel yourself being drawn to look at your circumstances that are contrary to your goal, immediately give it to God and confess His promise to "bring you to an expected end" (Jeremiah 29:11). When people seem to take an adversarial position to what God has called you to do, include Acts 4:29 in your prayer:

And now, Lord, behold their threatenings: and grant unto thy servants, that with all boldness they may speak thy word,

Stay prayerful and study the Word of God. Don't allow yourself to get distracted by the enemy who uses those in a weakened state to taunt you along your way. You have been predestined for a specific purpose at a specific time; follow your "marching orders" so you can be right where you are supposed to be and on time.

But the God of all grace, who hath called us unto his eternal glory by Christ Jesus, after that ye have suffered a while, make you perfect, stablish, strengthen, settle you (1 Peter 5:10).

Spiritual Success Gurantee

> *Grace and peace be multiplied unto you through the knowledge of God, and of Jesus our Lord, According as his divine power hath given unto us all things that pertain unto life and godliness, through the knowledge of him that hath called us to glory and virtue: Whereby are given unto us exceeding great and precious promises: that by these ye might be partakers of the divine nature, having escaped the corruption that is in the world through lust. And beside this, giving all diligence, add to your faith virtue; and to virtue knowledge; And to knowledge temperance; and to temperance patience; and to patience godliness; And to godliness brotherly kindness; and to brotherly kindness charity. For if these things be in you, and abound, they make you that ye shall neither be barren nor unfruitful in the knowledge of our Lord Jesus Christ. But he that lacketh these things is blind, and cannot see afar off, and hath forgotten that he was purged from his old sins. Wherefore the rather, brethren, give diligence to make your calling and election sure: for if ye do these things, ye shall never fall: (2 Peter 1:2–10).*

Christ has equipped us with a true understanding of what qualifies as Godly living. These characteristics must not only reside, but must increase, remain and mature as a constant in our conduct and daily behavior. When we continually demonstrate these virtues, we imitate Christ and like Christ, we experience unlimited guaranteed success. Take a close look into every one of these Christ like attributes, include them in your daily Christian walk and you will realize His purpose and the unprecedented favor He intended for your life.

Scriptual Firmness

> *Knowing this first, that no prophecy of the scripture is of any private interpretation. For the prophecy came not in old time by the will of man: but holy men of God spake as they were moved by the Holy Ghost* (2 Peter 1:20–21).

Believing this scripture has to be one of your most prevalent foundational beliefs before you can properly develop your Christian walk. No matter the opinions, you must stand and not waiver from the truth that the Bible is literally the spoken Word of God, written by men who were divinely influenced by the Holy Ghost. That's it and that's all!

Every other philosophy on this issue is no more than a deception to try to diminish the sovereignty of the only true, wise and living God. The Old Testament is the written Word of God as well as the New Testament; there is no separating of the two and everything God wrote will come to pass regardless of who does not believe. Jesus tells us in Luke 21:33:

> *Heaven and earth shall pass away: but my words shall not pass away.*

If anybody ever questions the authenticity of the Word of God, tell them what God says about His Word, and if they still don't believe, direct them to the author. God is willing to prove to them without a shadow of a doubt who He is and what He wrote if they're sincere and really want to believe.

Consolation

The Lord knoweth how to deliver the godly out of temptations, and to reserve the unjust unto the day of judgment to be punished: (2 Peter 2:9).

This conclusion is for inescapable temptations that defy reason and explanation. God has already determined the way, day, time, and hour of your deliverance and vindication. When justice seems to be nowhere to be found and you look more like the villain instead of the victim, remember, God's got your back. He's got you covered and He has you in the middle of His will and will not allow anyone to take you out!

My sheep hear my voice, and I know them, and they follow me: And I give unto them eternal life; and they shall never perish, neither shall any man pluck them out of my hand. My Father, which gave them me, is greater than all; and no man is able to pluck them out of my Father's hand (John 10:27–29).

Honest Relationship

This then is the message which we have heard of him, and declare unto you, that God is light, and in him is no darkness at all. If we say that we have fellowship with him, and walk in darkness, we lie, and do not the truth: But if we walk in the light, as he is in the light, we have fellowship one with another, and the blood of Jesus Christ his Son cleanseth us from all sin. If we say that we have no sin, we deceive ourselves, and the truth is not in us. If we confess our sins, he is faithful and just to forgive us our sins, and to cleanse us from all unrighteousness. If we say that we have not sinned, we make him a liar, and his word is not in us (1 John 1:5–10).

The fundamental building block to ensure a firm long lasting relationship must be honesty. Fellowship is sustained by having a commitment to be truthful and forthright in behavior and communication, this is what in turn establishes trust in a relationship.

As born again believers, we have been given the Word of God as the guideline for truth. These guidelines help to strengthen and maintain our relationship with Christ. God's Word shines brightly into the most obscure areas of our lives and exposes to us everything that's not like Him. When we agree with God and admit our guilt, and repent, He replaces our sins with His righteousness and forms us into what He has called us to be. We must be willing to live a yielded life of "yes" and allow God to mold us into His image. This surrender is a beckoning, that draws the paternal nature of God to bring His children to His protective side, and shield us from the world's lures to wander away again on our own.

Be willing to walk in the light exposure of God, for He is willing to cleanse you from the darkness of every secret sin and make you shine brightly with the righteousness from His Son.

Purified Hope

Behold, what manner of love the Father hath bestowed upon us, that we should be called the sons of God: therefore the world knoweth us not, because it knew him not. Beloved, now are we the sons of God, and it doth not yet appear what we shall be: but we know that, when he shall appear, we shall be like him; for we shall see him as he is. And every man that hath this hope in him purifieth himself, even as he is pure (1 John 3:1–3).

Mortal flesh is a work in progress and prone to its base nature, but yet and still God takes ownership of us. Now that's love! Not willing that we should be overwhelmed by our humanity, He gives us a reason to hope and a desire to change; to one day be just like Jesus and see God face to face. This is the goal of all His children, and is why we live holy, and look forward to the coming of our Lord and Savior Jesus Christ. There will be no more struggles with this flesh, and no more struggles with sin.

Corinthians 15:53 says:

For this corruptible must put on incorruption, and this mortal must put on immortality.

1 Thessalonians 4:16–18 further exhorts:

For the Lord himself shall descend from heaven with a shout, with the voice of the archangel, and with the trump of God: and the dead in Christ shall rise first: Then we which are alive and remain shall be caught up together with them in the clouds, to meet the Lord in the air: and so shall we ever be with the Lord. Wherefore comfort one another with these words.

Let the hope of Christ's coming motivate you to be ready when He comes. Be encouraged and:

look up for your redemption draws nigh (Luke 21:28).

Sacrificial Giving

> *Hereby perceive we the love of God, because he laid*
> *down his life for us: and we ought to lay down our*
> *lives for the brethren. But whoso hath this world's*
> *good, and seeth his brother have need, and shutteth*
> *up his bowels of compassion from him, how*
> *dwelleth the love of God in him?* (1 John 3:16–17).

Sacrifice is a character marker of love! When love attaches itself to giving it supernaturally metamorphoses your ordinary giving into sacrificial giving. Sacrificial giving gives until the sacrifice has been satisfied. If God says give away your suit, you give away your suit. If God says give away your new suit, you give away your new suit. If God says give away a few new suits with the shoes to match, guess what? You're right! You give away the shoes and the suits.

Now the great thing about sacrificial giving is that God honors and rewards you not only with the peace of obedience, but He also replaces everything with more than and better than.

So don't ever be afraid to give when God asks you to give, remember:

> *for God loves a cheerful giver* (2 Corinthian 9:7).

> *In this was manifested the love of God toward us,*
> *because that God sent his only begotten Son into*
> *the world, that we might live through him.*
> *Herein is love, not that we loved God, but that*
> *he loved us, and sent his Son to be the propitiation*
> *for our sins. Beloved, if God so loved us, we ought*
> *also to love one another* (1 John 4:9–11).

Perpetual Love

Ye are of God, little children, and have overcome them: because greater is he that is in you, than he that is in the world. They are of the world: therefore speak they of the world, and the world heareth them. We are of God: he that knoweth God heareth us; he that is not of God heareth not us. Hereby know we the spirit of truth, and the spirit of error. Beloved, let us love one another: for love is of God; and every one that loveth is born of God, and knoweth God. He that loveth not knoweth not God; for God is love (1 John 4:4–8).

As God, love doesn't have a beginning and will never end. Love existed before He created us and will continue throughout eternity. God has shown us His love and placed it within us to replicate and love continually as He loves. The love of God is not a one time "act of kindness", but a lifestyle of opportunity and commitment. God has been loving for a very long time, join Him and live a love lifestyle; let's love one another as a display of the love God has for us.

This is my commandment, That ye love one another, as I have loved you (John 15:12).

Seeing ye have purified your souls in obeying the truth through the Spirit unto unfeigned love of the brethren, see that ye love one another with a pure heart fervently (1 Peter 1:22).

Being born again, not of corruptible seed, but of incorruptible, by the word of God, which liveth and abideth for ever (1 Peter 1:22–23).

Perfect Love

And we have known and believed the love that God hath to us. God is love; and he that dwelleth in love dwelleth in God, and God in him.

Herein is our love made perfect, that we may have boldness in the day of judgment: because as he is, so are we in this world.

There is no fear in love; but perfect love casteth out fear: because fear hath torment.

He that feareth is not made perfect in love.

We love him, because he first loved us.

If a man say, I love God, and hateth his brother, he is a liar: for he that loveth not his brother whom he hath seen, how can he love God whom he hath not seen?

And this commandment have we from him,

That he who loveth God love his brother also (1 John 4:16–21).

A mature, complete love walk repels and terminates fear and trepidation. Love and fear cannot co-exist; they are diametrically opposed to each other. Love invalidates and cancels the rationale of fear. Perfect Love is not conditional or subjective, it is solely predicated upon its originator; God, and this premise; He is love, so we love. Perfect love is obtainable, but you must go to the source to get it. Don't settle for an imitation, get the real deal, a full, complete, and boundless love.

Heard/Answered Prayers

And this is the confidence that we have in him, that,
if we ask any thing according to his will, he heareth
us: And if we know that he hear us, whatsoever we
ask, we know that we have the petitions that we de-
sired of him (1 John 5:14–15).

The first appeal in the prayer the Lord taught His disciples in
Matthew 6:10 is

Thy kingdom come. Thy will be done in earth, as it
is in heaven.

This emphasizes God's priority for His will in us on earth. We
have been instructed that praying God's will gives us an audience
with Him, and if He grants us audience, He grants our request.

The Holy Ghost assists us in how to pray God's Word and
His Will. Romans 8:26 tells us:

Likewise the Spirit also helpeth our infirmities: for
we know not what we should pray for as we ought:
but the Spirit itself maketh intercession for us with
groanings which cannot be uttered.

Our flesh tries to intertwine our desires and include them in
the will of God. The Holy Ghost acts as a qualifier, inspects every
request, authenticates its validity, and rejects any illegal requests.

God knows our desires before we do. Psalm 139:4 reads;

For there is not a word in my tongue, but, lo, O
LORD, thou knowest it altogether.

Take the hint. God wants to tell you what to ask so He can
get to you what He wants you to have.

Total Prosperity

Beloved, I wish above all things that thou mayest prosper and be in health, even as thy soul prospereth (3 John 1:2).

God wants to be involved in every aspect of your life, so He can supernaturally bless you totally. His salvation is encompassing. It penetrates the spirit, transcends to the physical, and overflows to the financial to permanently impact and transform your life to His Word.

This is His plan for you; do not allow doubt and unbelief to short change you from God's "exceeding great and precious promises" (2 Peter 1:4). As a born again believer you are entitled to every blessing in the Word of God, so search them out and by faith receive them and watch your life become conformed to total prosperity.

Maintaining Faith

> *Beloved, when I gave all diligence to write unto you of the common salvation, it was needful for me to write unto you, and exhort you that ye should earnestly contend for the faith which was once de-livered unto the saints* (Jude 1:3).

Living in this world is challenging. Living a Christian life in a society driven by human secularism is even more challenging. Aggressively pursue and proclaim the power of the Word of God through love and faith. Feed your faith, study, pray and seek God's face daily. Guard your ear, eye and mind gates, don't allow anything contrary to holiness to enter into your thoughts and you will be the victor and possessor of a consistent and well maintained faith in God.

> *But ye, beloved, building up yourselves on your most holy faith, praying in the Holy Ghost, Keep yourselves in the love of God, looking for the mercy of our Lord Jesus Christ unto eternal life. And of some have compassion, making a difference: And others save with fear, pulling them out of the fire; hating even the garment spotted by the flesh. Now unto him that is able to keep you from falling, and to present you faultless before the presence of his glory with exceeding joy, To the only wise God our Saviour, be glory and majesty, dominion and power, both now and ever. Amen* (Jude 1:20–25).

And again,
I say
AMEN!